印象中国十九世纪

Images of 19th Century China

中英对照

编著 ／ 裘国英

Edited by Alan Chiu

上海文化出版社

SHANGHAI CULTURE PUBLISHING HOUSE

作者简介

裴国英，1949 年出生于上海市，台湾辅仁大学化学系毕业，企业经营者，爱好音乐、摄影及古籍收藏，曾游历全球五十多个国家，经常观察国际政治及撰写相关文稿。除《印象中国十九世纪》外，将陆续推出同时期有关印度、埃及、中东、欧洲、美洲等英文版的类似书籍，以期对历史建筑景观印象之保存，提供贡献。

About the Author

Chiu Kuo-Ying（Alan Chiu），born in Shanghai in1949, was graduated from chemistry department of Fu Jen University, Taiwan. He is now an entrepreneur, interested in music, photography and collecting antique books. He has also travelled more than 50 countries all over the world, observing political situation and writing commentary. He, besides published this book <Images of 19th Century China> will publish other books relating ancient India, Egypt, Mid-East, Europe and America one after another, in a hope to make a contribution to preserve images of historical architectures and landscapes.

目 录 Contents

导 读

重现 19 世纪的
历史面貌

李鸿章曾以千年来未有之大变局来形容 19 世纪中国所面临的问题，但 20 世纪及 21 世纪的中国变化更为巨大。传统家族制度逐渐崩解，男女臻于平等，女子受教育及工作者愈来愈多；农业虽为根本，但工商蓬勃发展，传统的市集逐渐被大的百货公司及卖场所取代，人口逐渐往城市集中。文化方面，传统的儒家思想自清末及五四运动以来遭到极大的挑战，西方思潮如狂潮巨浪席卷整个中国。在一连串的变化中，有些给中国带来正向的发展，有些则带来极大的破坏或改变，许多珍贵的文物流失，许多伟大的建筑被战火所破坏。重构历史的面貌，成为我们这一代人的使命与责任。

如何重构 19 世纪中国的面貌，除了档案、史料、回忆录、出土文物之外，最重要的是图像，包括照片、绘画、版刻等，这些图像具有赏析的作用，更有助于历史建筑的重建。然而，这些材料既稀有亦不容易取得，裘国英先生戮力搜集古籍，此次搜集的 19 世纪的刻印画英国画家 Thomas Allom（阿龙）的画作，内容多元而精致，有助于我们了解 19 世纪中国的各种风貌。

裘国英先生是辅大化学系毕业，是成功企业家的典范，热爱历史、热心公益、提携后进，并且有执行力，平时喜欢搜集古籍、周游各国，具有世界观，此次搜集 19 世纪中国的刻印画，不仅保存，且将之出版流通，对于保存史料贡献卓著。

本书主要以 Thomas Allom 的作品为主，他是 19 世纪大英皇家建筑师，在伦敦设计

导 读
Preface

0I3

了许多建筑物，包括圣彼得教堂和诺丁山优雅的 Ladbroke 庄园。1843 年在英国出版《图说中国帝国》（The Chinese empire illustrated，有些翻译成《百年前的中国》），这本书一问世，立即成为英国，乃至欧洲以绘画本呈现中国历史的教科书，是西方主流社会了解中国的主要读物。当时欧洲人关于中国的知识，许多是从这部书中获得，中国较有名的圆明园、长城、景山、午门、运河、虎丘塔、雷峰塔、报恩寺、琉璃塔、金山寺、龙舟、灯笼、宴请、婚礼，乃至祭拜、掷骰子等都经由这本书流布于欧洲。

Thomas Allom 的版画比用相机拍摄更美，刻画的内容相当丰富，到处都是古老中华帝国的风光、建筑及社会习俗。有上层统治者的生活记录，如道光皇帝大阅兵、官员府邸、官老爷出巡等；有庶民生活，如通州卖茶和卖猫商人、迎亲队伍、天津大剧院、端午龙舟赛、卖菜船工与鸬鹚捕鱼、养蚕人家等；有中国重要建筑，如大报恩寺琉璃宝塔、鼓浪屿、万里长城、北海公园、南京古城等，这些版画不仅可以让读者了解当时中国的官宦富豪居住之精美，还可一窥庶民生活的况味，带领我们进入 19 世纪中国各地的情境，犹如一部 19 世纪中国的精美旅游手册。画中有许多建筑基于战火或其他因素现已不复存在，如南京大报恩寺琉璃宝塔、厦门城门牌楼、南京古城、乍浦古桥等，虽经修建，然与 19 世纪时期的实景仍有一段落差，这些版画有助于重现当时历史的面貌。

林桶法
辅仁大学历史系教授兼系主任

Preface

Reappearance of Historical Images

Li Hongzhang, a premier in late Qing Dynasty had a word describing great changes in 19th century as "changes never been seen in 1000 years", but China saw much more greater changes in 20th and 21st centuries, including: political system has altered, traditional family line has collapsed, men and women have enjoyed equal social status, more and more women have an access to education and job opportunity, industry and commerce have grown vigorously,traditional fair trade has been replaced by department stores and supermarkets,and peasants have moved gradually into cities. As to culture, Confucius doctrine had been seriously criticized and western culture had entered prevailing all over the country. In fact, some of them had created positive effects, but there also brought about great damages to China, e,i, a lot of precious Chinese culture relics had been lost and washed away, and countless historical architectures had been destroyed. Now it is a duty of us to let the lost images reappear.

But how to realize the reappearance? We could depend archives, historical materials, memoirs and unearthed relics, among them. however, the most important part is pictures, including photos, paintings and wood-or-metal cuts, that could help reconstruct the lost historical architectures and landscapes, but this kind of pictures were difficult to seek and acquire. Now, Mr.Chiu Kuo-Ying(Alan Chiu) made great effort to collect Thomas Allom's, a British painter in 19th century, cut-and-print pictures that contained various aspects of subject and made possible for us to realize how Chinese people's life was like in 19th century.

Mr.Chiu Kuo-Ying(Alan Chiu) was graduated from the chemistry department of Fu Jen University. He is a successful entrepreneur with strong management ability, interested with passion in history, concerning public events and willing to help youngsters. He is also interested in collecting ancient books, travelling round the world that made him have a wide view to observe world events. He has collected the cut-and-print pictures about Chinese life style in 19th century, and now decided to publish them. This publication would be a contribution helpful for China preserve historical materials.

This book contains mostly Thomas Alloms' works. He was a British royal architect in 19th century, and has designed many architectures in London,as well as S. Petersburg Church and the Ladbroke Manor at pretty Notting. In 1843, he published a book *The Chinese Empire Illustrated*, and it soon became a text book from which people in England and all over Europe could understand Chinese life style in vivid images. During the time, the westerners mainly from this book got the knowledge about China, like: famous Yuanmingyuan Palace, the Great Wall, Jing Hill, the Noon Gate, the Great Canal, the Tiger Hill Pagoda, Leifeng Pagoda, Bao'en Temple, Glass pagoda, Jin Shan Temple, dragon Boat, lantern, banquet, wedding, kowtow and throwing dice, etc.

Thomas Allom's cut-and-print pictures were really more beautiful than photos,showing rich contents about ancient sights of China empire, architecture and social custom, including: 1, imperial and high officials' activities, like Emperor Daoguang reviewing troops,officials' residence, and their outing patrolling. 2, common people's life style, like vendors selling their tea and cats in Tongzhou City, wedding parade, TianJin Great Theater, dragon boats competition, selling vegetable boat, cormorants catching fish and a family raising silk worms. 3,Chinese important architectures, like glass pagoda at Bao'en Temple,Gulangyu Island, the Great Wall, the Beihai Park, ancient city wall of Nanjiang. These pictures provided us a variety of views about not only the elegance and beauty of Chinese high class residence, but also the situation of common people's day-to-day life. They served us as a guide book leading us to travel and sightsee all over the country in 19th century. More, many scenic relics had now disappeared or been destroyed due to the elapse of time or wars, like the glass pagoda at Bao'en Temple, the decorated archway in Xiamen, ancient wall of Nanjing and an ancient bridge in Zhapu. Though some of them had been rebuilt, the new ones actually look different from the original ones. In this case, the pictures could help us recover them back to their original style in 19th century.

Lin Tongfa
Professor and leader of Histry Department
of Fu Jen University

自　序
古董刻印画里的
历史实境

2016 年中美南海海域冲突事件发生时，我在网络上想找一张地图，希望能证明中国对该海域的长久主权，哪怕是找到一张洋人印制的中国地图都行。结果找到早自 16 至 17 世纪，西洋人到中国来探寻而写的游记，有德文、荷兰文、法文版本，虽然看不懂，但书中的插画极为有趣，反映出当时的山川景物，以及民间生活，更有趣的是，当时西洋的画家画中国人，画出来的都是西洋人身材、西洋脸，但穿着的是中国服装。

那时照相术尚未问世，有钱的大佬到各地游历，带着画家，看到有趣的景物，就画下来，算是对当时的中国，作了珍贵的写实记录。我们看到博物馆中收藏的中国古画，写意较多，用足够透视感画写实的较少，尤其是从西洋人眼中看东方、看中国，似乎从画里仍透露出他们的惊艳与好奇。

继续搜索中，在网络上结交了在欧洲从事古董书画买卖的人士，出于热心也是生意，他们代我搜集类似的书籍和零散插画，我将其命名为"古董刻印画"。

这些画的制作程序是，先由画家将画完成，交给雕刻师，雕在木头、石头或钢板上，再由印刷工匠，一张一张印出来，画上往往留下画家和雕刻家的姓名。这种刻印画早期都用木板制版，纹理较粗，但到 19 世纪，大概炼钢技术已较为成熟，因此开始刻在铜板上，这样的效果明暗立体乍现，连画中人物的脸部明暗，身上衣着的刺绣，建筑物梁上的花鸟都能表现出来。

19世纪的刻印画出现最多的画家要属英国的 Thomas Allom，我给他个昵称叫"阿龙"。其实阿龙是个建筑师，许多伦敦的名邸都出自他手，他也是英伦建筑师学会的创办人。

阿龙的画，内容遍及欧洲、中东、亚洲各地，估计他跑了不少地方，后来因在艺术及建筑上的成就，被封为爵士。阿龙画了不少建筑景观，由于他对透视度的重视及擅长，阿龙画中的建筑，比用相机拍的建筑物更美、更夸张。从画中，能让我们了解到当时中国社会的百态，有些画面让人有身临其境之感。

19世纪末，照相术成熟了，人们开始用照相取代手绘，雕刻艺术家及印刷工匠逐渐放弃了这一行当，但是他们所留下的版画是十分珍贵的，因为历经岁月、战争的侵蚀和破坏，许多建筑、景物已不复存在，具象的历史只能进入版画的空间，用思想去游历了。

裘国英

2017年夏

Historical Practice in Antique Steel Plate engraving Paintings

When the conflict between China and the US happened about SouthChina Sea water territory in 2016, I wanted to search on the web to find a map that could testify China had a sovereign right over the area, perhaps a map been painted by some westerners. I then found a lot of travelling notes written by westerners who travelled in China in 16th and 17th centuries, in languages of German,Holland and France, Though I couldn't read them, I was interested in many illustrated paintings showing geographical situation and social life style. more interesting that the Chinese people painted in the pictures were westerners, only wearing Chinese clothes.

During that time, the photo technique had not appeared, when some rich men went out travelling, they often took a painter with them, painting down interesting things they met on route. and the paintings had become precious record of realities of ancient China. In museums, people could now see Chinese traditional paintings, and they were used brushwork skills, instead of using western skills. I found that when the western painters in that era painted China or other eastern countries , their paintings also revealed their feelings of astonishment and curiosity.

I continued to search on the web, made friends in Europe engaging antique trade. They, out of enthusiasm and trade, have collected for me the same kind of books and illustrated pictures which I named them as the antique steel plate engraving pictures.

The process of making the steel plate engraving picture was like that: at first the painter finished his work, and gave it to the carving artist, who carved the image on a wood or metal plate, and then the printing worker printed the picture out. Usually the painter and caving artist's names were left on the picture.In early days, the pictures appeared rough veins as they mostly used wood plate,until in 19th century, the artists began to us metal plate that greatly improved the pictures' quality, which could reveal shadows on people's faces, embroidery on clothes and carved flowers and birds on the roof beams.

The most part of pictures I collected were painted by Thomas allom's works.(I gave him an intimated name as A Long) In fact, A Long was a architect and had resigned many famous architectures. He was also the founder of the Architects Institute of London.

The subjects of A Long's paintings involved places in Europe, Mid-East and Asia, proving he had travelled a lot of countries. Afterward,he had been offered an title of duke due to his contributions on architecture and arts. A Long had painted many architecture landscaped. He was good at perspcctive skill, so, the images in his paintings were more beautiful than photos, showing us a variety of social life phenomena of ancient China that could make us feel being personally on the scene.

By the end of 19th century, the photography technique appeared, making the carving artists and printing workers gradually gave up their jobs, but they left behind valuable works. As many architectures and ancient relics had already disappeared by the elapse of time or been destroyed in war fire, these pictures could really provide people to sight-see the beauty of ancient life style by imagination.

Chiu Kuo-Ying(Alan Chiu)
Summer 2017

推荐语
Recommendations

古董刻印画其精致的雕工，严谨的复制，自然不在话下，我们还可把它当作是一部有画面的中国历史读本。借由画中的各种场景，肯定会带给我们更多的想象空间。

王懋勋
南加州伶伦剧坊前社长及导演

The elegance and strictness of the paintings are surely to be admired, and we could regard them as the history text books of ancient China which could provide us more space for imagination.

Michael M.Wang
Former President and Director of Southern California Ling Luen Drama Club

本书中收录许多极为珍贵的古董雕刻画，描述清朝时代的中国人文与文化。由画中的风景、建筑、社会风俗可以体会当时的民生。而画中呈现着西方人眼中的中国，又值得玩味，引人入胜，令人着迷。

李小雅
生物化学博士

The book had collected a lot of high valuable antique steel plate engraving paintings which display Chinese society and culture in Qing Dynasty, and providing people to understand architectures and social custom in that era. In addition, these paintings, due to reflect westerners' observing China, appear more fascinating and amazing.

Hsiaoya Lee
PhD Biochemistry scientist

此书的问世，不啻是刻印画收藏者的福音，也是近代历史研究者的瑰宝，更给世人带来两三百年前，我们祖辈们生活的点点滴滴。

刘政平
美华航天工程师协会创会会长

The publicity of the book is the Gospel for the collectors of the steel plate engraving paintings. It is also a treasure for the researchers of modern history. More, it brings about for people vivid images of our ancestry's day-to-day life two or three hundred years ago.

Stephen C. Liu, P.E.
Founder of Society of Chinese American Aerospace Engineers(SCAAE)

近百张精美的版画，栩栩如生地表现出 19 世纪初期中国社会的人文百态。Thomas Allom 善用透视构图与写实的光影变化，让画中的人物、建筑与风景产生令人震撼的视觉感受。

陈重裕
美国阿克隆大学高分子科学博士

Near 100 elegant steel plate engraving paintings reveal vividly various views of day-to-day life of Chinese society in early 19th century. Thomas Allom was skillful to use perspective and reality painting technique, and the images of persons, architecture s and landscapes in his paintings make people produce feelings of amazing and shaking.

Dr, Chen Joungyei (Frank)
PhD, Polymer Science，University of Akron, USA

道光皇帝大阅兵

The Parade of Emperor Daoguang

清文宗道光皇帝每年元旦都要在北京的皇宫检阅八旗禁卫军。兵部要将领勇猛如虎,将领为士兵披上虎皮,并且在盾牌上画上猛兽的图案。

阅兵式上只见八旗军官头戴闪亮头盔,顶部插着一根大约八英寸的羽冠,装饰着金顶和花翎,他们身穿蓝色或紫色丝袍,脚蹬黑缎做的靴子,刀剑的手柄、弓的弯角和火绳枪的枪托镶着闪亮亮的宝石。各式旗幡迎风招展,士兵抬着轿子,打着灯笼,举着龙旗,皇家乐队现场演奏,锣鼓喧天,还有形状像是龙、蛇、鱼的吹奏乐器,伴着不计其数的竖笛和琵琶。

Emperor Daoguang during Qing Dynasty reviewed the "Eight Banners" Guards every New Year's Day in the Royal Palace in Beijing. Generals of the Ministry of War in feudal China were as brave as lions and they covered soldiers with tiger skins, painting beast patterns on their shields.

The parade witnessed the officers wearing shiny helmets, with about 8 inches of feathers on the top, decorated with golden tops and HuaLings (a kind of peacock feather). They are wearing blue or purple silk robes and black satin boots. Shiny bright jewels are inlaid in the handle of the sword, the corner piece of bows and the gunstock of matchlocks. All kinds of flags are fluttering in the wind. Soldiers are carrying sedan-chairs and holding lanterns as well as dragon flags. The live royal band performs with gongs and drums. There are some wind instruments in the shape of dragons, snakes and fish, accompanied by countless clarinets and pipas.

Drawn by T. Allom.

Engraved by J. B. Allen.

The Emperor "Teaou-Kwang" reviewing his Guards, Palace of Peking.

L'empereur Teaou-Kwang passant ses gardes en revue
Palais de Peking.

Der Kaiser Teaou-Kwang hält Parade seiner Garde
vor dem Palast zu Peking.

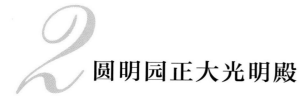

圆明园正大光明殿

The Open and Above Aboard Hall in the Yuanmingyuan Palace

19世纪的中国，大清帝国威仪天下，北京城里巍峨的宫室、栉比的府第错落有致，经常接待外国藩使的圆明园尤为富丽堂皇。占地十一平方英里的公园里，假山池沼、流觞曲水与超过三十组的独立宫殿浑然一体。

建筑在四英尺高花岗岩台阶上的正大光明殿，四周环以红漆圆木支撑着檐顶，内排柱子的间隔部分砌着四英尺高的砖墙，砖墙上方镶着格子框架，框架里糊着高丽纸，可根据气温变化自由开关。宫殿地面的工艺简单朴素，铺着漂亮的灰色地砖，呈棋盘式排列。大殿正中，鎏金龙椅雄踞，门前放置两面大鼓，皇帝驾到时，随即咚咚响起。

The 19th century of China is during the period of Great Qing Empire with an impressive and dignified manner all over the world. In Beijing, lofty palaces and row upon row of scattered houses were well organized. The Yuanmingyuan Palace became even more magnificent and gorgeous owing to reception of foreign emissaries. In the 11-square-mile park, the rockery mountain, the pond and the winding stream integrated with over 30 independent palaces perfectly.

The Open and Above Aboard Hall, built on four feet tall granite steps, is surrounded by logs painted in red to sustain the canopy top. The intervals of the inner row of pillars are filled with four feet tall brick walls, on which are decorated with lattice frames made by Hanji (a kind of Korean paper), switching freely according to the temperature change. The craft of the palace ground is simple and austere, arranged like the checkerboard with beautiful grey floor spreading on it. The golden dragon chair is standing stately in the middle of the hall. In front of the door are placed two big drums, which would be played when the emperor arrived.

Drawn by T. Allom.

Engraved by E. Brandard.

Hall of Audience. Palace of Yuen min Yuen, Peking.

Salle d'audience, Palais de Yuen min Yuen, à Pékin.

Audienz Saal, Palast von Yuen min Yuen, Peking.

3 虎丘山帝王行宫

The Open and Above Aboard Hall in the Yuanmingyuan Palace

苏州城西北约九华里之处的山丘间，坐落着虎丘山帝王行宫。这幅画中央的岩石壁上写着"虎丘"二字，就是此处的地名。

虎丘之名由来，相传是因为春秋时代吴王阖闾葬于此处，下葬后第三天有人看见一只白虎盘踞在墓碑上好几天，而且每年定期造访。据传，当秦始皇想毁掉吴王墓时，这只白虎就会出现。因为这个历史典故，加上此处风景优美，吸引了秦朝官员王珣和王珉在峡谷里建造了别墅。行宫的后面有岩石跨越深谷与对面的崖壁相连，崖顶上是美丽的虎丘宝塔，宝塔原本是河神庙的一部分，塔上视野开阔。

The 19th century of China is during the period of Great Qing Empire with an impressive and dignified manner all over the world. In Beijing, lofty palaces and row upon row of scattered houses were well organized. The Yuanmingyuan Palace became even more magnificent and gorgeous owing to reception of foreign emissaries. In the 11-square-mile park, the rockery mountain, the pond and the winding stream integrated with over 30 independent palaces perfectly.

The Open and Above Aboard Hall, built on four feet tall granite steps, is surrounded by logs painted in red to sustain the canopy top. The intervals of the inner row of pillars are filled with four feet tall brick walls, on which are decorated with lattice frames made by Hanji (a kind of Korean paper), switching freely according to the temperature change. The craft of the palace ground is simple and austere, arranged like the checkerboard with beautiful grey floor spreading on it. The golden dragon chair is standing stately in the middle of the hall. In front of the door are placed two big drums, which would be played when the emperor arrived.

Drawn by T. Allom.

Engraved by J. Sands.

The Imperial Travelling Palace at the Hoo-kew-shan.

Le Palais Impérial de Hoo-kew-shan.

Der kaiserliche Reise Palast zu Hoo-kew-shan.

4 官老爷出巡

The Officer Patrol

披着帷幕，缀着流苏的轿子，一张交织着银线的丝网覆盖在轿顶，顶部装饰圆球。两根竹竿穿过轿子两侧的锁扣，用绳索连在一起，另一根短的竹竿从绳索下面穿过，短竹竿的两端扛在轿夫的肩膀上，四个轿夫分摊了轿子的重量，当他们显露疲态，还有另外四个轿夫跟在一旁，随时准备换班。

一群仆人走在轿子前，有的敲锣，有的吆喝，提醒闲杂人等让路，还有一人拿着棍子威吓周围看热闹的民众。到达目的地，向前递上红色长简，若是受访者正在办丧事，则用写上蓝色字体的白色竹简。这就是官老爷出巡，若是皇帝出巡，则是八人大轿，再配上穿黄制服的骑兵护卫。

Dressed in curtains and tassels, the sedan has a silk net intertwined with silver wires covering and the decorative ball on its top. Two bamboo rods come through locks on both sides of the sedan, connecting with each other by the rope. Below the rope comes across another shorter rod, both ends of which are shouldered by bearers. Four bearers share the weight and when they get tired, another four bearers will follow and be ready to shift.

A group of servants walk in front of the sedan: some beat gongs and others shout to remind people to let the way. What's more, there is a person with a short stick to alert the populace surrounding, who are watching the bustling. When reaching the destination, someone will step forward to send the red slip. If respondents are during the funeral period, then the slip will be the white slip with blue words on it. This is the officer patrol. When it comes to the emperor patrol, the sedan will become the larger one with eight bearers, matched with cavalry guards in yellow uniforms.

Drawn by T. Allom.

Engraved by A. Fox.

A Mandarin paying a visit of Ceremony.

Mandarin rendant une visite de cérémonie.

Ein Mandarin der einen förmlichen Besuch abstattet.

官家宅院

The Official House

中国官员的宅院环绕着湖水荡漾，镶花格木柱支撑着华美建筑，右边迎宾楼的双层屋顶令人惊艳。从阳台上放眼望去，中间一座大气宽敞的拱桥横跨，拱桥上方还能看到高高的宝塔矗立，屋顶以倒扣的莲花钟为形状。

19 世纪的中国人喜欢用与佛教相关的物品如莲花、瓷瓶、灯笼、神像来装饰，还将桑叶形状装饰在门廊和窗扉上。若说佛教是心灵所依，桑叶则是吐丝蚕儿的必要食物，而丝绸为中国贡献国库所需。

这张插画其实取材自皇亲安利波家族的府邸，从阳台和花架使用"特拉法加式"来装饰，一部分还模仿扭曲的树枝，可以想见主人兴建府邸时的用心。

The house of Chinese officials is around the rippling lake, with wooden lattice pillars supporting the gorgeous building. The double-layer roof of the guesthouse on the right side is amazing. Looking out from the balcony, you can see a big arch bridge stretching across the lake in the middle, behind which stands a tall pagoda. The roof resembles an upside-down lotus bell.

Chinese in the 19th century enjoy decorating with some Buddhist-related items such as lotuses, porcelains, lanterns and statues of Buddha. They also decorate porches and windows with mulberry leaves. Buddhism is what the soul depends on, just like mulberry leaves are what silkworms depend on and silk is what the contribution to Chinese treasury depends on. This ikon is actually based on the house of royal family Anlibo. Judging from the decoration of balconies and flower racks using "Trafalgar" style and the part imitation of twisted branches, we can imagine the devotion of the host to the construction.

Drawn by T Allom.   Engraved by A. Willmore.

Pavilion and Gardens of a Mandarin.
near Peking.

Pavillon et Jardin d'un Mandarin près de Pékin.   *Pavilion und Garten eines Mandarins. bei Pékin.*

官员府邸

The Official Residence

盘发以金簪或银簪固定，额头上装饰着头带。太太坐在镶着丝绸刺绣的竹制椅子上，老爷抽着烟威武站立一旁，奶娘也带着孩子聚拢过来，一位商人展示着货物努力推销。

从官员府邸的建筑与宅内的装修风格看，更能真实了解中国人的生活方式。尽管建筑的外部装饰及华丽程度比不上古希腊罗马，住所的格局却意外地非常相似。大厅、庭院、门廊到卧室的通道虽然狭窄又曲折，外面的院墙也很容易翻越，但习俗和习惯，以及司法效率，却让这座官员宅邸比想象中还要安全许多。

With the hair fixed by the golden or silver hairpin and the forehead decorated with the headband, the wife is sitting on the bamboo chair embroidered with silk, the husband is smoking and standing beside, the wet nurse is bringing children to gather together and a businessman is showing around and promoting his products.

We can get to know the actual lifestyle of Chinese according to the internal and external decoration style of the residence. Although the exterior decoration and its luxury degree are no match for those in ancient Greece and Rome, their arrangements of the residence are very similar by accident. The hall, the courtyard and the road from porch to bedroom are narrow and filled with twists and turns, but the external wall is easy to climb. Fortunately, this residence is safer than expected owing to customs and habits as well as judicial efficiency.

Apartment in a Mandarin's House, near Nanking.

Appartement dans la maison d'un mandarin, près de Nankin.　　Zimmer in dem Hause eines Mandarins, bei Nanking.

7 官府宴客

The Official Banquet

相较于节俭的百姓之家，清朝官员的官邸就像一间间艺术品博物馆。无论是餐厅或是房间里的家具都很名贵，墙壁和天花板上装饰着原木细工雕刻的浮雕，壁纸色泽鲜艳。

就连一张桌子也是巧夺天工，摆上各式装饰品，中央放着玻璃、陶瓷或白银制作的雕花托盘，插着鲜花和熏香的瓷瓶则置于其上。雕花椅子也是重要的角色，上面置放的丝绒刺绣或天鹅绒垫子和靠垫，衬托不凡格调，坐在餐桌正面的主人，座椅还比客人的座位高一些。

宴会期间一定有戏班子在房间的另一头等着出场，文戏过后的各种蹦跳腾空武戏和杂耍，总会带动起现场宾客的阵阵喝彩。

Compared with the relatively frugal common house, the official residence in Qing Dynasty is like an art museum. Whether the dining room or the furniture in the room are luxurious. On the walls and ceilings are decorated with relief delicately graved with logs and wallpaper with bright colours.

Even the table is wonderfully artical excelling nature, on which all kinds of decorations are put. In the middle of the table are laid carved trays made of glass, ceramic or silver, with fresh flowers in it. Aromatherapy porcelains are also placed on it. Carved chairs also play an important role, on which are placed with velvet embroideries or velvet cushions. In order to emphasize the extraordinary one, the host sitting on the right side of table has a higher seat than the guest.

During the banquet, there must be a troupe waiting for the appearance on the other side of the room. After the Chinese opera follows various martial arts and juggling shows, leading to bursts of applause from guests.

Dinner Party at a Mandarins House.
China.

Dîner de cérémonie chez un Mandarin.

Gastmahl im Hause eines Mandarins.

8 官宦女眷的生活娱乐

Entertainment for The Womenfolk of The Official Family

官宦女眷的房间里，通常会有一个拜神的空间，壁龛里摆着神像，一幅刺绣的丝绸帘幕垂在神龛前。画中的女眷坐在神像前，认真地打着牌，作为排遣生活无聊的方式。

19 世纪的中国贵妇，生儿育女是她们的主要职责，一般情况下，孩子稍大点就会被送到私塾学习文化。白天孩子不在身边，这些贵妇只好以其他方式填补生活空虚。平时若家里只有两个女人，就下下棋，两人以上，最受欢迎的活动还是打牌了。

In the room of the official family, there is usually a space for worshipping the gods: the statues of the gods are placed in the shrine, in front of which hangs the embroidery curtain. The womenfolk in the painting are sitting in front of the statues and seriously playing poker cards, as a way of diverting themselves from a boring life.

As for Chinese women in the 19th century, they must observe the law if they want to bear children. If the son is at the age of 10, he must leave his mother and cannot enter the birthplace anymore. The law deprives women of taking the responsibility of being mothers. Hence, they have to pad their empty life in other ways. When they are allowed to see the child, their joy is palpable. If there are only two women at home, they will choose to play chess. If more than two, the most popular activity is playing cards then.

Drawn by T. Allom.

Engraved by A. Willmore.

Ladies of a Mandarin's Family at Cards.

Dames de la famille d'un mandarin jouant aux cartes.

Damen einer Mandarin Familie spielen Karten.

9 官家庭院里的杂耍表演

The Juggling Show in The Courtyard

当官员府邸的盛宴结束后，主人会带着宾客到宽敞的庭院，欣赏杂耍演员展现柔软身段或动作敏捷的表演。

在四周亭台楼阁之中，垂挂着华美灯笼，装饰着瓷器花瓶，满园花草芬芳。这些杂耍演员的演出令到访的友人惊叹，他们有时能脚串珍珠、口吞剑刃、两脚踩在装满水的大瓷碗和花盆上。或是让四五个圆球、杯子或刀子不断在空中回旋翻转，亦或是额头上放着杯子，再用脚不断转动圆环的杂技，有时也会表演魔术。

After the official banquet, the host will bring guests to the spacious courtyard to enjoy the juggling performance which shows the soft body and agile action of the juggler.

In pavilions and open halls around, there are gorgeous lanterns hanging, decorated with porcelain vases. The whole courtyard is filled with fragrance of flowers. Visitors marvel at the performance by jugglers. Sometimes they can string pearls by foot, swallow the blade into mouth and step on the big bowl or the flower pot filled with water. Sometimes they can enable four or five round balls, cups or knives to roll over and over in the air. Or they stack wood chips on their foreheads and then continue to roll the ring with their toes. Sometimes they can perform the magic.

Drawn by T. Allom.

Engraved by T. A. Prior.

Jugglers exhibiting in the Court of a Mandarin's Palace.

Jongleurs exécutant leurs tours d'adresse dans
le palais d'un Mandarin.

Taschenspieler im Hofe eines Mandarins.

大家闺秀的闺房

The Boudoir of Fair Ladies

19世纪上层阶级的夫人，总有一大群丫鬟簇拥着，当丫鬟忙着为夫人梳头，为她插上花饰或珠宝，夫人则悠闲地抽着烟，一旁坐着女乐师，弹奏着琵琶，以音乐丰富生活。

大家闺秀的闺房在府邸里，常常沿着起居室延伸或环绕着池塘，一条长长的回廊从起居室和花园通往阳台或门厅，房门口挡着一道丝帘，一掀开丝帘，里面就是闺房了。

在这些闺房中，总有一个柜子，里面装满化妆品、胭脂罐、扇子、鞋子、画笔和瓷瓶。雪白的肌肤，细且弯的眉毛，瑰红色的腮红和唇彩，是这些大家闺秀们的基本妆扮，她们想营造出百合与玫瑰的对比效果。

The upper class of ladies in the 19th century are always surrounded by a crowd of maids. When maids are busy with the hair of ladies including inserting floral decoration or jewelry, these ladies are just smoking leisurely. Beside them sit the female musician, playing the pipa to enrich their life.

The boudoir is in the official residence, always extending along the living room or surrounding the pond. A long corridor from the sitting room and garden leads to the balcony or hall. The curtain covers the boudoir inside.

In these boudoirs, there is only one cupboard filled with cosmetics, rouge cans, fans, shoes, brushes and porcelain vases. The white skin, the thin and curved eyebrows and the rosy blush and lipstick are their basic standards in order to create a sharp contrast between lily and rose.

Drawn by T.Allom.   Engraved by W. Floyd.

Boudoir and Bed-chamber of a Lady of rank.

Boudoir et chambre à coucher d'une dame Chinoise.   *Toilette und Bedzimmer einer vornehmen Dame.*

11 长城的尽头

The end of the Great Wall

险峻的山脉与波涛汹涌的大海对峙，万里长城绵延山峰与山谷，最后的尽头落在渤海之滨，位于河北省山海关城南四公里的老龙头，今日修筑了地标供人缅怀。但19世纪时，建造粗糙的平底商船航行至此，船上水手的安危只能听天由命。每年约有一万人葬身海湾，这些不幸事件让当地人有了忧患意识。他们做成了竹制的救生衣，竖起结实的桅杆，将甲板做成弧形，铺上更为防水的竹席，相信神明的影响力留置于罗盘中。于是在罗盘的背后设立小小祭坛，点燃一根用蜡、牛脂和沉香制成的小蜡烛，保持香火不断，借以象征神明的保佑。

Steep mountains are standing opposite the rippling sea. The Great Wall stretches along mountains and valleys, ending on the coast of Bohai Sea. The Old Dragon Head of the Great Wall, located in Shan-hai pass city of Hebei Province, is 4 kilometres far from the south of the city. Today this landmark is built for visitors to recall. However, in the 19th century, every time the roughly-built flat business ship sailed here, ship sailors could resign themselves to the fate. Almost 10,000 people were buried in the gulf of misfortune, which made the local aware of the danger. They would reinforce bamboos into life jackets, set up a solid mast and curve the deck which is covered with more waterproof bamboo mats. They believed that the influence of the deity will be left in the compass, so they set up a small altar behind the compass and lit a small candle made from wax, tallow and agilawood to keep the incense constantly, symbolizing the protection of deity.

Drawn by T. Allom.

Engraved by J. B. Allen.

Termination of the Great Wall of China, Gulf of Pecheli.

Fin de la grande muraille de la Chine, golfe de Pécheli.

End der großen Mauer von China, Golf Pecheli.

万里长城

The Great Wall

绵延五千英里，历经两千年的考验，长城始终屹立守卫着中国北方，若按平均每户需用两千立方英尺的砖瓦计算，建造整个英国住宅需要的材料都不比建造长城的材料多，两个数字的对照，让来访的英国人不禁赞叹起长城工程的无比宏大。

公元前二三七年统一中国的秦始皇所兴建的长城和北京几乎位在同一纬度，向东延伸至辽东湾，平均高度约二十英尺，其中护墙约五英尺，下砌十五英尺高的平台或壁垒。基座厚约二十五英尺，墙顶宽约十五英尺。墙身由外墙和内墙构成，空隙间填满了泥土、毛石和其他材料。垛墙高六英尺，墙面由花岗岩包砌，上面是青色城砖。台阶则是砖制或石制，可上至平台，亦可骑马拾级而上。

The Great Wall, stretching five thousand mile, is always standing and guarding the northern China through the test of two thousand years. If calculated at an average of two thousand cubic feet of tiles for every house, materials needed to build the whole British house are not as many as those to build the Great Wall. British visitors can't help but admire the grandeur of the Great Wall project and recall the past.

The Great Wall built in 237 BC by the first Emperor of Qin (Qin Shihuang) who unified the whole country the one in Beijing are almost at the same latitude. It goes eastward into the Far East Bay and its average height is about 20 feet, including about 5 feet parapet wall and 15 feet high platform or barrier below. The base is about 25 feet thick and the top of the wall is about 15 feet wide. The wall consists of the external and the internal wall. Soil, rubble and other materials fill the space between them. The stacking part of the wall, made of granite, is 6 feet high and its upper part is cyan-blue. You can mount on the platform or ride on the stairs which are made of bricks and stones.

Drawn by T. Allom.

Engraved by J. Sands.

The Great Wall of China.

La Grande Muraille de la Chine.

Die große Mauer in China.

北海公园

Beihai Park

这座始建于辽代的北海花园，是世界上现存建园时间最早的皇家宫苑。园内以环华岛为主体，岛的最顶端盖有永安寺白塔，这是清代顺治皇帝应喇嘛所请，将岛上广寒殿旧址改建而成，后来成为这座园林的象征。到了晚清内忧外患时刻，慈禧太后还曾动用海军军费维修这座心仪的园林。

画中的北海公园，湖边避暑别墅和凉亭楼阁掩映在怪石树丛之间，湖面往来穿梭着宫廷的游船，犹如一座快乐仙岛。

Built in the Liao Dynasty, Beihai Park is the oldest existing royal park in the world. The main part of the park is called Huanhua Island. On the top of the island is the white tower of Yongan temple which is converted from the old site of Guanghan Palace, asked by the Lama during Qing Dynasty governed by Emperor Shunzhi. It later became the symbol of this park. Even in the late Qing Dynasty during the state of flux, Emperor Dowager Cixi has used the navy fee into the construction of this park she admires.

In the painting of Beihai Park, summer villas and pavilions by the river are covered by stones and trees. With the royal boat shuttling in the lake, the park is like a happy fairy island.

Gardens of the Imperial Palace, Peking.

Jardins du palais impérial, à Pékin.

Schlossgarten zu Pekin.

西直门

Xizhimen

清代北京城，形状呈现长方形，北边的皇城供满族人居住，南边的老城或外城，则住着汉人。城的西面，共有阜成门、西直门、西便门、广安门四座城门，西直门位于西北，外国使节会经此门到圆明园。

每座城都有独立的围墙，外城占地九平方英里，皇城占地五平方英里，防御城墙高三十英尺，厚达二十英尺，采用老式建筑工法建成。就像英国兴建封建古堡，先筑两道土墙，石头底座，砖砌上面，外墙倾斜，内墙垂直，中间填土，不同的是，英国人用毛石，中国人用泥土和沙浆混合而成的混凝土。

Beijing in the Qing Dynasty is in the rectangular shape, with the north part for Manchu and the south or the outside of the city for the Hans. In the west of the city, there are four gates: Fuchengmen, Xizhimen, Xibianmen and Guanganmen. Xizhimen is located in the northwest, where foreign envoys will pass through in order to enter the Yuanmingyuan Palace.

Every city has its independent fencing wall. The outer city covers an area of 9 square miles, the royal city occupies 5 square miles and defense walls 30 feet high and 20 feet thick, built in an old way. It is just like the construction of the feudal castle in Britain: The first step is to build two walls with the stone base and bricks on it; the second step is to make external walls tilt and internal walls vertical in order to fill the middle part. The difference is that British fill it with clay while Chinese fill it with concrete made of clay and mortar.

Drawn by T. Allom.

Engraved by E. Brandard.

Western Gate, Peking.
China.

Porte de l'ouest à Pékin.

Westliches Thor zu Peking.

15 普陀山普济寺

Puji Temple in the Putuo Mountain

位于舟山群岛上的普陀山，是中国四大佛教圣地之一，这里的土地不过十二平方英里，本地人口不到两千人，却有超过三千僧侣居住于此。这座普济寺位于一座肥沃狭长的山谷里，两侧绝壁上的山峰高达一千英尺，两根高大的旗杆牢牢插入岩石中，旗杆之间的阶梯就是通往寺院的道路。

僧侣住的两层楼建筑，上面盘着几条龙，建筑后方一座宝塔，这里便是佛寺的大殿了。最特别的是，在这幅画中的右半部，有一座单碑式的十字架，这是明清两代欧洲商人留下的遗迹。

Located on Zhoushan Islands, Putuo Mountain is one of the four major Buddhist holy sites in China. Although the land is no more than 12 square miles and the local population is less than 2000, there are over 3000 clergies living here. The Puji Templeis located in a fertile and narrow valley, with both sides of cliffs 1000 feet high. Two tall flag poles are inserted into rocks tightly and the ladder between the flag poles is the road leading to the monastery.

Monks live in a two-story building, on which a few dragons wind. Behind the building is a pagoda and is the great palace of the temple. The most special is that: In the right part of the painting, there is a monumental cross, which is one of the remains left by European businessmen during Ming and Qing Dynasty.

Drawn by T. Allom. Sketched on the spot by Capt. Stoddart R.N. Engraved by R. Smith.

The Grand Temple at Poo-too, Chusan Islands.

Grand temple à Poo-too, Iles de Chusan. Der grosse Tempel zu Poo-Too, Chusan Inseln.

16 大报恩寺琉璃宝塔

The Glass Pagoda in Bao'en Temple

这座大报恩寺琉璃宝塔，有"天下第一塔"之称，明成祖朱棣为纪念生母贡妃而建。塔身高八十米，九层八面，周长百米，建造时间前后近二十年，匠人和军工达十万人，耗资二百四十八万两银子。清代康熙、乾隆到江南时均曾登临此塔，康熙皇帝曾为塔作诗，乾隆皇帝还逐层题写匾额。

这座塔于 1856 年毁于太平天国运动中，然据史书记载，建造此塔烧制的琉璃瓦、琉璃构件和白瓷砖均为一式三份，1958 年在附近出土了大批带有墨书字号标记的琉璃构件，现分藏于中国历史博物馆、南京博物院和南京市博物馆。

This glass pagoda in Bao'en Temple is known as "the world's first tower", built by the Ming emperor Zhu Di to commemorate his mother Gong imperial concubine. The pagoda is 80 metres high, with 9 layers and 8 sides. Its perimetre is one hundred metres. It has taken almost 20 years, 100,000 craftsmen and soldiers and 2.485 million silver dollars to construct this pagoda. During Qing Dynasty, both the emperor Kangxi and the emperor Qianlong have come to this pagoda. The emperor Kangxi once composed a poem for it, while the emperor Qianlong inscribed the plaque.

This tower was destroyed in 1856 because of the war of the Taiping Heavenly Kingdom. According to history, the glazed tiles, glass components and white tiles were all reserved in triplicate in order to build the pagoda. In 1958, great a many glass components marked by specific words were discovered, which are now stored in the Chinese History Museum, Nanjing Municipal Museum and Nanjing Museum.

Porcelain Tower, Nanking.

Tour de Porcelaine à Nanking.   Porcelain Thurm, Nankin.

镇江河口

Zhenjiang Estuary

这里是阻止敌国舰队前进的要塞，也是通往大运河的桥头堡，修建在木桩之上的码头或堤岸在大河上延伸出几百米远。货运帆船在此装卸或登陆，在河水不断冲刷的峭壁崖底修建了储存货物的仓库。

画中央是金山岛，松柏长得茂盛，宝塔和寺庙优雅耸立其上，岩顶上还有一排排白色屋子，是当地驻军的居所。出乎意料的是，其上方的土地十分肥沃，生产出的水果与蔬菜足可供应驻地居民。站在面朝北方的最高点，镇江码头与航运往来一览无遗。

Here is not only the fortress to prevent the enemy fleet forward, but also the key to the Grand Canal. The pier or embankment built on the stakes extend hundreds of yards away, where ships load cargo and land. The bottom of the cliff washed by the river constantly has built a warehouse for storing goods.

In the center of the picture is Jinshan Island with pines and pagodas, with temples standing gracefully on it. There are rows of white roofs which are local garrison's residences. Surprisingly, the top of the land is spacious and fertile, on which fruits and vegetables are enough for local residents. Standing on the top facing north, Zhenjiang port and shipping can be viewed at a glance.

Mouth of the river Chin-keang.

Embouchure de la riviere Chin-keang.   Mündung des Flusses Chin-keang.

镇江银岛

Zhenjiang Silver Island

比起高耸的金山，镇江银岛则自江面升起，深绿丰茂的植物遮住了银山的顶峰和两侧，小屋和别墅若隐若现。水深之处停满商船，维多利亚女王的船队就停靠在银岛之畔，而远处一支强大的分舰队便在镇江停泊。

这座"银岛"其实就是"焦山"，相传因东汉学者焦光在此隐居而得名。焦山的知名佛寺为"定慧寺"，古名"普济寺"，宋代嘉定年间一度易名"焦山寺"。清康熙年间，皇帝御赐"定慧寺"匾额，并加以修建，自此改名至今。苏东坡的方外之交佛印了元禅师曾禅修于此，乾隆下江南，也曾数度驻跸焦山，留下不少轶闻逸事。

Compared with the towering Jinshan, Zhenjiang Silver Island rises from the river. Green and thriving plants cover the peak and both sides of the silver mountain, with huts and villas looming. The depth section of water is full of merchant ships. The Queen Victoria's fleet landed near the Silver Island and a powerful sub-fleet landed on in Zhenjiang.

The Silver Island is actually Jiaoshan. This name originates from the hermit and the scholar Jiaoguang living here in Han Dynasty. The well-known Buddhist temple is Dinghui Temple whose ancient name is Puji Temple. During Song dynasty, it was changed into Jiaoshan Temple. During the Qing Dynasty (the Emperor Kangxi), the emperor granted the plaque "Dinghui Temple" and built the temple, becoming its name nowadays. Su Tungpo has a friend of monk whose name is Fo Yin and he is also called Liao Yuan Chan master .He meditated here.

The Emperor Qianlong once went to Jiangnan and spent much time in Jiao Mountain, leaving great anecdotes.

Yin-shan, or Silver Island, on the Yang-tse-keang.

Yin-shan ou île d'argent, sur le Yang-tse-keang.

Yin-shan, oder Silver-Insel, am Yang-tse-keang.

七星岩

Qixing Rock

　　远处耸立着高度达五千英尺的五峰山，近处在富饶的平原上，屹立着七星岩山体，两侧陡坡上点缀着农舍，周围的桑树和茶园，证明一群农民从平原地区迁居过来，这些人在裸露的岩石山群中求生。

　　下方是农民人工搭建的葫芦架，上面葫芦结实累累，这种被植物学家视为平常的植物，对于农民却大有用处。葫芦可食用，外壳也可用来当作水壶，就像左下方一位农民手里拿着葫芦水壶喝水一样。空葫芦除了喝水，还能在猎捕水鸟时用来伪装捕鸟者的头，这些伪装有时也放在水稻田中，以此阻遏鸟类啄食农作物。

　　Farther is Wufeng Mountain at the height of 5000 feet. Nearer are fertile plains, on which stand Qixing Rock. On both sides of steep slopes are dotted with farmhouses, surrounded by mulberry trees and tea gardens, proving that a group of farmers were excluded from the plains. These poorer people and new arrivals were forced to survive in bare rock mountains.

　　Below farmers build a gourd rack artificially, with abundant fruits on it. This kind of plant regarded as normal for botanists makes great contributions to farmers. Gourd is edible and its shell can be used as a kettle, just like one farmer in the lower left corner holding gourd in his hand and drinking. In addition to drinking water, it can also disguise the head of the bird when hunting the waterfowl. These disguises are sometimes put in rice fields.

Tseih Sing Yen, or The seven-star Mountains

Tseih Sing Yen. ou les Montagnes des sept étoiles.   Tseih Sing Yen. oder sieben Sternen Gebirge.

20 湖州的丝绸庄园

Silk Manor in Huzhou

远处耸立着高度达五千英尺的五峰山，近处在富饶的平原上，屹立着七星岩山体，两侧陡坡上点缀着农舍，周围的桑树和茶园，证明一群农民从平原地区迁居过来，这些人在裸露的岩石山群中求生。

下方是农民人工搭建的葫芦架，上面葫芦结实累累，这种被植物学家视为平常的植物，对于农民却大有用处。葫芦可食用，外壳也可用来当作水壶，就像左下方一位农民手里拿着葫芦水壶喝水一样。空葫芦除了喝水，还能在猎捕水鸟时用来伪装捕鸟者的头，这些伪装有时也放在水稻田中，以此阻遏鸟类啄食农作物。

Located in the tributary of the Grand Canal and near the Huzhou Mansion, here is the so-called "silk area" by the Chinese geographer. Due to the beautiful scenery on both sides of the lake, many rich people are attracted to settle down. The painting depicts a mansion owned by a rich silk estate owner. The surname of the manor owner is Liu and his whole family live here from generation to generation. When the raw silk in the storage room accumulates a certain amount, it will be loaded in flat boats with bamboo sheds, sailing towards the canal. He doesn't care about who bought the silk, but care about how to create a more cozy circumstance for the manor with money earned.

Royal robes also come from silk produced in this region. Rich officers also come here to order products for the whole season. Even foreign businessmen boast that they can distinguish between silk here and silk from other regions in China.

Drawn by T. Allom.

Engraved by J. Tingle.

Silk Farms at Hoo-Chew.

Fabriques de soie à Hoo-Chew.

Seiden Pachtgut zu Hoo-Chew.

21 定海郊外

Dinghai Suburbs

定海是一个人口稠密的古老贸易城市，当地有蛮荒之地，也有农耕地区，还有先朝古迹和名人墓碑。郊外矗立着一座巨大牌楼，牌楼前，一座平坦的桥梁横跨溪流两岸，周边长满灌木和杂草。当地随时有表演艺人在街头演出，民众也会在这里举行佳节盛会，以音乐、戏剧和食物来感谢神明，表演者聚集在临时搭建的棚子里。当举行各种节庆游行时，总会吸引众人前来定海。

Dinghai is an ancient trade city with dense population. There are undeveloped regions and farming areas in the local. What's more, there are historical sites and celebrity monuments as well. Outside the suburb stands a high decorated archway, in front of which a flat bridge crosses over the stream, surrounded by shrubs and weeds. In the local, there are street performances by artists at any time and the populace hold and celebrate festivals here. They express their gratitude for the deity by the means of music, drama and food. Performers gather in the temporarily built shed. When a variety of festivals were held, people are attracted all the time to Dinghai.

Drawn by T. Allom. Engraved by S. Fisher.

Scene in the Suburbs of Ting-hae.

Vue dans les faubourgs de Ting-hae. Scene in der Umgegend von Ting-hae.

乍浦古桥

The Zhapu Ancient Bridge

　　地处杭嘉湖平原的乍浦镇，在宋、元两代曾开港贸易，设立市舶司。由于地形倚山面海，形成海防要地，明嘉靖年间和清道光年间在此曾经发生抵抗倭寇和英军的战役，导致乍浦数度被毁。这幅画清晰地描绘了19世纪的乍浦镇，镇上一座连接乍浦河的单孔石板桥吸引着游人的目光，因为这座桥属于平拱桥，在桥梁建筑工法里最为古老。做法是先在两边修建牢固的桥墩，像楼梯一样层层重迭地铺设大石板，一直铺到河边，再按所需尺寸将大石板铺在两边桥墩的跨河空间上，石桥的栏杆上有一尊一尊做工不甚精细的石狮子。

　　Located in the Hangjiahu plain, the Zhapu Town once started the port trade and set up the Shi-Po-Si during Song and Yuan Dynasty. As the terrain leant mountains and faced the sea, it became coastal defense. During Ming Dynasty (Jiajing) and Qing Dynasty (Daoguang), battles happened here to resist the Japanese pirates and the British, destroying Zhapu many times. This painting depicts the Zhapu Town in the 19th century clearly, in which a single-hole slate bridge attracted the British because this bridge belonged to the flat arch bridge almost and was the oldest in the construction of the bridge. How to construct it: build a solid bridge pier on both sides. Lay and overlap large slates like stairs, which can be paved to the riverside. Then lay slates on both sides of the bridge pier over the river. There are many stone lions which are not so delicate on railings of the bridge.

Drawn by T. Allom. Sketched on the spot by Captⁿ. Stoddart, R.N. Engraved by R. Sands.

Ancient Bridge, Chapoo.

Ancien pont, Chapoo.   Alte Brucke, Chapoo.

秦淮古桥

The Qinhuai Ancient Bridge

　　此画描绘的是南京秦淮河上的长干桥，始建于唐朝，明代一度改名长安桥，清代称聚宝桥。这座优雅的单孔桥，石头被切割成圆孔的一段，不用楔形石，而是将木头　入桥孔凸面，再用铁闩穿过石头，将其牢牢固定在桥上，将弯曲的石头榫接成较长的横向石块，再用小一点的石头砌成圆形桥孔。

　　大桥修建在结实的砖石桥墩上，全部用花岗岩建成，圆形桥孔由楔形石头砌成。大桥两侧修建了住宅，成群结队的牛群、马车和齐步前进的军队，都撼动不了这座桥的稳固性。画中一艘皇家御船已经抵达，船上载着前来与外国人交涉的钦差大臣。

　　This painting depicts Chang-gan Bridge over Qinhuai River in Nanjing. Originally built in the South Tang Dynasty, this bridge was renamed as Chang'an Bridge during Ming Dynasty and then Jubao Bridge during Qing Dynasty. As for this elegant single-hole bridge, the stone is cut into part of a round hole. Instead of wedge stones, the wood is embedded into the convex bridge hole, with the iron bar passing through the stone in order to fix it tightly to the bridge. Curved stone tenons are connected to a longer horizontal stone piece, while the smaller stones are built into round bridge holes. The big bridge is built on a solid pier made of granite and round bridge holes are all made of wedge-shaped stones. On both sides of the bridge are dwellings. Even crowds of cattle, carriages and the army stepping forward together can't shake the stability of the bridge. In the painting, a royal ship has arrived, on which an imperial minister is coming to negotiate with the British.

Drawn by T. Allom.   Sketched on the spot by Capt. Stoddart. R.N.   Engraved by J. B. Allen.

The Bridge of Nanking.

Le Pont de Nanking.   *Die Brücke zu Nanking.*

西湖

The West Lake

西湖湖岸长约二十英里，突出的岬角与凹进的港湾交错有致，宁静清澈的湖面点缀着两座林木葱郁的小岛，最古老也最显眼的，莫过于雷峰塔。

岸边土地肥沃，吸引来自城里的官吏、富豪来此定居。从西湖岸边到山脚下形成宽阔盆地的险峻山峰，每一个地方都布满别墅、宫殿、寺庙、戏园和花园。无论白日或黑夜，西湖里荡漾着许多游船。

连绵不断的寺院、豪宅、树林和花园，甚至墓葬群，都围绕着这片美丽的大湖。其中，纪念碑和坟墓的设计各有千秋，达官贵人即使往生，也要与其他人有所区别，他们在半圆形平台上修建坟墓。

The West Lake is about 20 miles long and the bulging promontory is staggered with recessed bay. The tranquil and clear lake is dotted with two islands with thriving forests. The most ancient and conspicuous is Leifeng Pagoda.

The soil near the bank is fertile, attracting officials and the rich from the city to settle down here. From the shore of the West Lake to dangerous mountains forming a wide basin at the foot of the mountain, every place is full of villas, palaces, temples, theatres and gardens. Whether in the day or at night, the West Lake is squeezed by cruise ships with different levels.

Continuous temples and monasteries, mansions and villas, wood and gardens and even tombs surround this beautiful big lake. Among these, designs of monuments and graves both have their merits. Even though the rich and officers die, they need to be separate from others. They build tombs on the semi-circular platform.

Drawn by T. Allom.   Engraved by J. C. Bentley.

Lake Sée-Hoo and Temple of the thundering Winds, from the Vale of Tombs.

Le lac Sée-Hoo de la vallée des tombeaux.   Sée Sée-Hoo und Tempel der donnernden Winde.

25

南京古城

Nanjing – An Ancient City

  南京是中国四大古都之一，向来是国家重要的教育中心，明清时期中国许多的状元出自南京的江南贡院。鸟瞰南京，可以对中国人的社会结构和城市街道布局有大致的了解，它们方方面面都规规矩矩。这幅南京全景图，图中可见一边是高山峻岭，从山上可俯瞰整座城市和近郊的景致，另一边则是密布着住宅，长长的柏油路从城门直通长江边上。城市的西南角是衙门所在，那里有一道水门，通过一座横跨运河的四孔桥。向东被城墙围起来的部分是瓮城，越过城堡往北，还可见到陡峭的小山。

  Nanjing, as one of the four oldest cities in China, is always the centre of education and science. During Ming and Qing Dynasty, more than half of the literature champion were from Jiangnan examination hall in Nanjing. Having a general view of Nanjing, we can roughly know about the social structure and the city layout that all aspects are under regulation. In this picture of Nanjing panorama, we can find that one side is full of mountains overlooking the scenery of the city and suburb. The other side is full of dwellings. The seven-mile-long asphalt road stretches from the gate to the riverside. The government office is located in the south-west of the city, where there is a Watergate through a four-hole bridge across the canal. The urn castle is surrounded by walls in the east and the farther in the north are steep hills.

Drawn by T. Allom.　　　Sketched on the spot by Capt. Stoddart, R. N.　　　Engraved by E. Radclyffe.

Nanking, from the Porcelain Tower.

Nanking, vu de la tour de porcelaine.　　　*Nanking, von dem Porcelain-Turm gesehen.*

江南寒泉山

The Cold Spring Mountain in Jiang-nan

寒泉山距离苏州城西二十里，那里气候清爽，风景如画，研究中国艺术的人通常认为此处是抒情诗人最该造访之处。寒泉所属的太平山脉，矿藏与植被物十分丰富。幽深山谷、悬崖峭壁、高耸山峰和大瀑布尽在其中。平地拔起的寒泉山，为苏州城抵挡劲风，犹如一道屏障壁垒。所谓寒泉山，即为现今苏州天平山的白云泉。白居易有诗咏此泉曰："天平山上白云泉，云自无心水自闲。何必奔冲山下去，更添波浪向人间。"

"On the lofty summits, where the white clouds rest, the milky source is elevated; The fountain didn't intend to writhe, rushing down the mountain and gathering new power; It appears in the full tide of majesty when it comes within the sight."20 miles away from Suzhou, the Cold Spring Mountain has a clear weather and a picturesque scenery. Those who study Chinese art all recognize here to be the place lyric poets visit most frequently. As for the Taiping mountain range the Cold Spring belongs to, mineral and vegetation are themes for writers, including deep valleys, cliffs, towering peaks and great waterfalls. The Cold Spring Mountain springing up resists the fierce wind for Suzhou, like a barrier. The so-called Cold Spring Mountain is the White Cloud Fountain in Tianping Mountain in Suzhou.

Han-tseuen,— Province of Kiang-nan

Han-tseuen.— Province de Kiang-nan.　　　　Han-tseuen.— Provinz Kiang-nan.

27

浙江富春山

Fuchun Hill in Zhejiang Province

富春山又名"严陵山"，是东汉名士严子陵隐居、垂钓的地方。山腰有二盘石，称东西二钓台，各高百余米，巍然对峙，耸立江湄。周围崇山环抱，蓝天白云，山清水秀，旁边还有一些池塘。钱塘江从这里的群山中夺路而出，奔向大海。一道瀑布从山间飞流直下，水潭犹如一面巨大的镜子倒映着周遭的美景。

严子陵何许人也？他是东汉光武帝刘秀尚未登基时的朋友，家财万贯，学问造诣颇高。当光武帝登基后，多次征召其担当谏议大臣，严子陵婉拒，并归隐富春山。

Fuchun Mountain, also known as "Yanling Mountain", is the seclusion and fishing place where the famous bachelor Yan Ziling lived. Surrounded by mountains, the blue sky and white clouds, the West Lake, the Saint Lake, Lingyun and Tangyang River are all scattered here, with some ponds beside. Qiantang River takes the road from mountains here and runs towards the sea. A waterfall between mountains fly down. The pool looks like a gigantic mirror, reflecting the charming scenery.

Who is Yan Ziling? He is the friend of Liuxiu when he was still the prince before he became the emperor during Eastern Han Dynasty (25-220) Yan Ziling was not only wealthy, but also made great achievements in knowledge. When the Emperor Liuxiu came to his throne, he secluded in Qi (a state during this period). Under the great hospitality of the Emperor Liuxiu, he entered the imperial court to serve as the imperial advisor, but the prime minister Hou Ba at that time scrupled him. Yan Ziling knew the sinister officialdom well, so he quitted his job and secluded in Fuchun Mountain.

Drawn by T. Allom.

Engraved by J. C. Bentley.

The Foochun Hill, in the Province of Chè Keang.

Colline de Foochun dans la province de Chè Keang.

Der Foochun Berg in der Provinz Chè Keang.

太湖碧螺峰

The Biluo Peak in Taihu Lake

位于江苏省南部和浙江省北部交界处的太湖，是中国五大湖泊之一，临近太湖东岸星罗密布着许多小岛。湖边群山环绕，山脉沿着湖边绵延好几英里，其中碧螺峰最为知名，相传碧螺春茶之名因此峰而来。

居民在山脚下修建了别墅和农场，两座宝塔在岬角与岩石小岛上左右矗立，只有货运帆船往来时，才会打破暂时的宁静。这里贸易兴盛，货船会运出棉花，运进从杭州经大运河而来的外地农产品。由于利润丰厚，当地建立了税务衙门，衙门前竖立着圆柱和黄龙旗作为标志。

Taihu Lake, located at the junction of the south of Jiangsu Province and the north of Zhejiang Province, is one of the five biggest lake in China. Near the east coast of Tai Lake is dotted with many small islands, surrounded by mountains extending several miles along the lake. Among these mountains, the Biluo Peak is the most well-known. The name of the peak originates from the tea name: Biluo-chun tea.

Residents at the foot of the mountain built villas and farms and two pagodas respectively stand in the headland and on the rocky island. Only cargo ships coming back and forth can break the temporary tranquility. The trade here is prosperous: cargo ships will export cotton and important agricultural products from Hangzhou through the Great Canal. Owing to abundant profits, the local tax government office was established, in front of which were set up cylinders and yellow dragon flags as a sign.

Drawn by T. Allom.

Engraved by J. Sands.

The Polo Temple, Tai-Hou.

Le temple de Polo à Tai-Hou.

Der Polo Tempel zu Tai-Hou.

瓜岛水车

Waterwheels on the Gua Island

　　赣江支流流经瓜岛，进入鄱阳湖，瓜岛平原上可以看见上百部水车。仔细观察过中国的竹制水车，外国人发现，原来全世界最早的水车发明者应该是中国农民，因为其制作原理与埃及水车极为相似，年代却更早。粗大的短竹筒的一端被堵死，它们平均间隔被固定在水车轮网的外侧，水车不需要保持精确的水平状态，在转动的过程中，以某个角度来装水，再将水倒进准备接水的水槽。水车作为汉族农耕文化的重要组成部分，它体现了汉民族的创造力，为中国农业文明和水利史研究提供了见证。

　　The branch of Gan River passes the Gua island and flows into the Poyanghu Lake. On the plain of the Gua Island can see hundreds of waterwheels. Every waterwheel can pump 3 million tons of water every day. After observing Chinese bamboo waterwheels carefully, the British have discovered that the original inventor of the waterwheel in the world should be the Chinese farmer as Chinese and Egyptian principles of production are similar but China invented it earlier. One end of the thick short bamboo is blocked. The average interval is fixed outside the wheel felly of the waterwheel. The waterwheel doesn't need to maintain a horizontal state precisely, but it can be filled with the stream water in a specific angle precisely. In the process of circling, water is always held and is poured into the water sink.

Drawn by T. Allom.

Engraved by H. Adlard.

Melon Islands, and Irrigating Wheel.

Iles des melons et roue d'irrigation.

Melonen Insel und Bewässerungs Rad.

 石门

The Stone Gate

河流两岸陡峭崎岖，巍峨的山峰直上云霄。当船顺流而下，水流速度加快，尤其到达两根擎天巨柱旁，行船人稍不谨慎，随时都有可能撞上礁石。这里就是石门了，周边地区石灰岩随处可见，在河的另一侧，还有一种角砾岩。

两边的石柱让航道宽度变窄，形成内凹，此处河水深邃，可遮风避雨，给商船提供了一处安全的码头。此画是石门的直观印象，当时的游吟诗人，用大胆艳丽的语言描绘游石门所历经的三种不同景色，从美轮美奂到庄严肃穆，最后是惊恐震慑。

River banks on both sides are steep and rugged and towering peaks goes up to the sky straightly. When the boat goes down with the river flow, the water speed becomes faster. Especially when reaching two gigantic stone pillars, boatmen tend to hit rocks if they are not careful enough. Here is Shimen (Stone Gate). Limestones surrounding can be seen everywhere. On the other side of the river, there is also another kind of breccia.

Stone pillars on both sides narrow the width of the channel, forming the concave. The river here is so deep that it can shelter people from wind and rain and provide a safe ship dock. This painting reflects the direct impression on the Stone Gate (Shimen). The local poet describes three different sceneries with gallant words after travelling, from the magnificent view to the solemn view and finally turning into shock and awe.

Drawn by T. Allom.

Engraved by Le Petit.

The Shih-Mun, or Rock-Gates.
(Province of Kiang-nan.)

Le Shih-mun ou barriere de Rochers.
(Province de Kiang-nan.)

Die Shih-Mun oder Felsen-Thore.
(Provinz Kiang-nan.)

31 焦山行宫

Jiaoshan Palace

相较于金山，焦山地势更为陡峭，地貌也更丰富。登焦山必须爬上长长的阶梯，山上环境清雅幽绝，人称诗、书、画三绝的郑板桥亦曾于雍正年间在后山别峰庵作画读书。

焦山比金山更为有名，是因为焦山的石碑典藏，在史料和书法艺术方面都有很高的价值，蜚声海外，被誉为"书法之山"。其中，被称为碑中之王的《瘗鹤铭》，相传为东晋大书法家王羲之所书，原刻在焦山崖石上，宋朝时受雷击而崩落于长江之中。清朝康熙五十一年，镇江知府陈鹏年派人从江中捞起，仅存八十六个字，其中不全的有九个，但仍可见潇洒苍劲的字迹。

Compared with Jinshan, the terrain of Jiaoshan is steeper and the landform is more abundant. There is a long ladder to climb up Jiaoshan. The circumstance on the peak is quiet and tranquil. Zheng Banqiao, who is famous for his poems, books, paintings during Qing Dynasty once painted and read during the period governed by the Emperor Yongzheng in the Biefeng hut behind mountains.

Jiaoshan is more famous than Jinshan on account of stone collections, whether judged by historical materials or calligraphy arts, which are renowned overseas. Henceforth, Jiaoshan is known as "Calligraphy Mountain". Among these works, the king is called "Yihe Monument", which is said to have been written by the great calligrapher Wang Xizhi during the Eastern Jin Dynasty. The original one is curved on the Jiaoshan cliff, but it was fallen into the Yangtze River owing to the lightning strike. In the 51st year governed by the Emperor Kangxi during Qing Dynasty, Zhenjiang magistrate Chen Pengnian sent someone to pick it up from the river, only remaining 86 words, in which 9 words are incomplete. However, we can find the shape of the word is vigorous.

Drawn by T. Allom.   Engraved by F. W. Topham.

Imperial Palace at Tseaou-shan.

Le Palais Impérial à Tseaou-shan.   *Kaiserlicher Palast zu Tseaou-shan.*

扬州渡口

Yangzhou Ferry

历史悠久的古城扬州，气候宜人、风景如画，商业活动发达，对于欧洲人来说，这里的天气犹如意大利南部和地中海的西西里岛。当地民众对家中的闺女从小就让她们学习歌唱、绘画和演奏乐器，期望有一天能登上豪华堂会表演。也因此，扬州无论音乐、诗歌、绘画和通俗文学都得到良好的发展。

画作描绘的地方是位于长江与古运河交汇处的瓜洲渡，石桥上方的山岩上有戏园、凉亭和古朴的剧院。夜晚到来，人们结束工作返回住所，许多人通过石桥过河，也有一些人用小船来摆渡。

The ancient city Yangzhou with a long history has an agreeable climate, a picturesque scenery and developed commercial activities. As for the European, the weather here is similar to that in the south of Italy and the Sicily Island in the Mediterranean. Local people educate their daughters to be perfect when they are small, such as teaching them sing, draw and play musical instruments. They expect their children to perform in the luxury hall one day. Therefore, whatever music, poetry, painting or popular literature can be developed well.

This painting depicts the Guazhou Crossing Ferry, located at the intersection of the Yangtze River and the Ancient Canal. On rocks over the stone bridge are gardens, pavilions and quaint theatres. When the night arrives, tens of thousands of people return to their residences after their work. Hence, the stone bridge can't hold crowds of people and many people cross over the canal by boat.

Drawn by T. Allom.   Engraved by A. Willmore.

The Pass of Yang Chow.

Détroit de Yang Chow.   Der Engpass zu Yang Chow.

33 远眺宁波城

Overlooking Ningbo

位于甬江和姚江交汇处，地理位置便利，享有天然良港的优势，宁波港的对外贸易比其他一般的港口要来得多，当时从这里出口丝绸、棉花、茶叶和漆器，以交换外国的羊毛和武器。

宁波城的周围是绵延数英里的平原，边界上高山耸立，因此形成巨大的椭圆形盆地，小镇星罗棋布。这里的土壤肥沃，灌溉工程便利，使得农作物繁茂丰收，有大米、棉花、豆类等。远眺宁波城，犹如一幅美丽的图画。

Located at the junction of Yong River and Yao River, Ningbo has always more foreign trades than other free ports with its convenient geographical location and its advantage of the natural harbor. Silk, cotton, tea and lacquerware are exchanged for wool and weapons in Britain.

Surrounding Ningbo are plains stretching several mile. In the distance mountains stand, thus forming a gigantic oval basin. The small town is dotted. The land here is fertile and the irrigation is convenient. Water flows into 66 irrigation channels directly from surrounding mountains, moisturizing the whole land and making crops rich and productive including rice, cotton and beans. Overlooking the whole Ningbo, it is like a beautiful painting.

Drawn by T. Allom.

Engraved by S. Bradshaw.

City of Ning-po, from the river.

Ville de Ning-po, vue de la rivière.

Die Stadt Ning-po, vom Flusse.

34 五马头山

Five Horses Heads Mountains

珠江流域第二大水系的北江，发源于江西大茅山，干流在韶关市区以上称浈江（也称浈水），韶关以下始称北江。北江流经虎门时，由于长期冲刷，一侧的石崖间冲出一条水道，与另一侧的石灰岩彷佛要挨到一起，形成一个高耸的拱形洞穴。在这个峡谷航行并不十分安全，因为石灰岩有时会从悬崖往下掉，日积月累阻塞了河道。船只若在此处触礁沉没，由于两侧全是悬崖峭壁，根本无法逃生。在当地一个被称为"五鬼把门"的河段，经常可以看到一些船只的残骸。画中的五座山峰犹如五个马头。

North River, the second largest river in the Pearl River basin, originates from Damao Shan in Jiangxi Province. After containing Wu water right in Shaoguan, it is then called as North River. When the North River passes through Humen, one side of cliffs flows out of a channel, while the other side of the limestone seems to gather together, forming a towering arch cave. Sailing in this canyon is not safe because the limestones will sometimes fall down from the cliff and block the river over time. If ships strike the reef and sink here, it's impossible to escape because both sides are cliffs. The local river called "Five Ghosts Hold the Door" is full of wreckages of vessels. In the painting, five mountains are like five horse heads.

Drawn by T. Allom.

Engraved by W. Floyd.

The "Ou-ma-too", or Five Horses' Heads.

L'"Ou-ma-too", ou les Têtes des Cinq Chevaux.

Der "Ou-ma-too", oder fünf Pferde Köpfe.

THE LONDON PRINTING AND PUBLISHING COMPANY _ LIMITED

35 广州街道实景

The Actual Scenery of Guangzhou Streets

　　此画真实描绘了广州城市中央一条商店街的概况。密集的建筑、花岗岩铺设而成的狭小街道，适合步行或乘坐轿子通过，不适合四轮马车行驶，犹如英国伦敦的石板庭院和过道。在欧洲人眼中，广州的大街除了拱廊上的玻璃帷幕外，其他的地方也可与巴黎的相比。走不多远，便会看到一道活动木门或铁门，门后的警卫室里住着守夜的警卫，这些人奉命守护每一条街道，担负防火、防盗和维护治安的责任。

　　商家的货物摆在店外，顾客可以自由挑选，橱窗或门边放置商家标志，象征店主的名号。街边摆设着竹制大伞，商人就在伞下与顾客交易。

This painting is a true description about a business street in the centre of Guangzhou. Dense buildings with narrow streets paved by granite were only suitable for walk or sedans except four-wheel carriages. It was like the stone courtyard and aisle in London. From the perspective of the European, the arcade except for the glass curtain on it on Guangzhou Avenue could be compared with the Paris Arcade. Not far away, a loose leaf or iron gate could be seen, behind which was a guard room with guards throughout the whole night. These guards followed the order to protect every street and take the responsibility for preventing fire, thieves and maintaining security.

Merchants' goods were placed outside shops for customers to select freely. Next to showcases or doors were business logos, symbolizing the reputation of owners. Bamboo umbrellas were arranged on the street, so that businessmen can trade under them.

A Street in Canton.

Rue, à Canton.

Eine Strasse in Canton.

珠江黄塔

Yellow Tower in Pearl River

　　此画是珠江一处热闹的河岸，四周环境赏心悦目。河岸的一侧有一栋漂亮的别墅藏身树林间，浓密的枝叶掩映着它，门前有一段宽阔的阶梯；另一侧则是寺庙，围墙里有一座高高的宝塔，经过的船只会在此处停歇，船员下船到寺庙里祈求航程平安。各种驳船、帆船、小船和货船密集地排在河岸边上，新到的船根本无法停靠，必须藉由警察的协助才有办法。在这样的环境下，船只间稍有碰撞，就有可能引起纷争，造成人身伤害，一直等到宁波口岸通商后，类似的状况才得以缓解。

　　The closer the Pearl River was to Guangzhou, the more vibrant vitality you could feel. Shops, houses, business villas and dark residential intercourses on both banks were staggered. This painting is about a lively riverbank, surrounded by satisfying circumstances. There is a beautiful villa hiding among trees on one side of the river. With dense foliage, in front of the door is a wide ladder. On the other side is the temple and there is a high pagoda behind walls. Ships passing will stop and rest here and the crew will get off to pray for a safe journey. A variety of barges, sailings, boats. Cargo ships and large boats line up on the riverbank. New ships couldn't stop at all except the assistance by the police. Under such situations, a slight collision between ships would cause disputes and lead to the personal injury. This condition got better until the port of Ningbo started the trade.

Pagoda and Village, on the Canal near Canton.

Pagode et village sur le canal près Canton.　　　　　*Pagoda und Dorf am Canale bei Canton.*

西樵山

Xiqiao Mountain

由于丰富物产，广东成为南方最富饶的省份，除了精致的工艺品外，这里还有黄金、宝石、丝绸、珍珠、沉香、水银、锡、铜、铁、糖、钢、硝石、乌木和香料等，当地的商业气习浓厚。

此画为 19 世纪时的西樵山，位于广州市西面约一百英里的珠江三角洲上。这座状似一条浮龙的西樵山，雏形来自四五千万年前的火山喷发，大量熔岩形成的西樵山的七十二座奇峰，直耸天际，清幽秀丽，还有奇峰怪石和流泉飞瀑，姿态万千。此画左下角有一渔民驾着平底船，用精心编织的渔网捕鱼，这是西樵山居民最稳定的职业之一。

Owing to abundant products, Guangdong becomes the richest province in the south area. In addition to exquisite handicrafts, mountains contain gold, gems, silk, pearls, incense, mercury, tin, copper, iron, sugar, steel, saltpeter, ebony, a large quantity of spices and etc. The local commercial atmosphere is very full.

This painting is Xiqiao Mountain in the 19th century, located on the Pearl River Delta, about 100 miles west of Guangzhou. The Xiqiao Mountain, like a floating dragon, comes from a volcanic eruption about 40 or 50 million years ago. A great amount of lava forms 72 unique mountains, straight towering the sky as well as quiet and beautiful. There are other unique mountains, stones and waterfalls with hundreds of thousands of images. In the lower left corner of painting, a fisherman is driving a flat boat and fishing with a delicate well-woven net. This is one of the most stable occupations for residents in Xiqiao Mountain.

Drawn by T. Allom.

Engraved. by J. Redaway.

Se tseaou shan, or "The western seared hills."

Se tseaou shan, ou les Montagnes brûlés de l'ouest.

Se tseaou shan, oder westliche verdorten Hügel.

38 海幢寺的码头和入口

The Pier and Entrance of Haizhuang Temple

位于广州珠江南岸的海幢寺，一边连接着狭小的街道，另一边连着海上仙岛，游客最爱到这里求神拜佛。寺院紧邻江边，码头上常年人头攒动，船只往来频繁。寺庙门口的建筑，包括山门、屏风、山墙、挑檐、凹顶和怪兽，给人一种乡村酒馆的感觉。这里是通往菩提树林的入口，过了树林之后，沿着石板路，便是海幢寺了。

聚集于码头上的人群，在来访的欧洲人眼里，显得有些奇怪，他们中的一些人只是对着一块木头膜拜，希望死后在阴间不会遭受到刀叉斧钺之刑。

Located in the south bank of the Pearl River in Guangzhou, Haizhuang Temple connects to the narrow streets and attaches to the fantastic Island in the sea, which is the favorite place for visitors to pray here. The monastery is close to the river. The pier is always crowded with people, with frequent ship exchanges. The construction in front of the temple gate includes the gate, the screen, the gable, eaves, the top and the monster, leaving people a feeling of the country pub. Here is the entrance to the Bodhi woods, behind which is Haizhuang Temple.

The crowd gathering on the pier, from the perspective of the European visiting, were both inferior and humble. These European even suspected their beliefs, believing that these people were just worshipping towards a piece of wood and were hoping not to be punished by swords and axes after their death in the underworld.

Drawn by T. Allom.

From a sketch on the spot by Warner Varnham, Esq.

Engraved by C. T. Dixon.

Landing Place and Entrance to the Temple of Honan, Canton.

Débarcadère et entrée du temple d'Honan, à Canton.

Landungs. Platz und Eingang zum Tempel Honan.

海幢寺

Haizhuang Temple

这是中国南方最知名的寺院，走进广场便可看见三座大殿，里面供奉着许多尊神像。最重要的中间大殿里，供奉着三尊大佛，每尊高约十英尺，以坐姿呈现，称为三世佛，亦即佛祖的三位一体，象征过去、现在和未来佛。三座金佛前都摆上一张祭台，上面放满各种供奉用品，有香炉、线香、熏香、杯子、鲜花、花瓶和奇珍异果，两旁站着十八罗汉，两边墙上装饰着帷幕，用金银丝线绣了许多儒家箴言。寺院里还设有僧侣的房间，按照修道等级分配。

This is the most famous monastery in the south of China, in which three main halls can be seen with many statues inside. What's the most important, three deities were served, which are about 10 feet high. They came to appearance in the sitting way. They were called Buddhas of Three Periods, meaning the Trinity of the Buddha and symbolizing the past, the present and the future. In front of three gold Buddhas were placed an altar, on which were all kinds of incense, cups, flowers, vases and peculiar fruits, with eighteen disciples of the Buddha standing beside. On both sides of the wall are decorated with curtains which are made of gold or silver thread embroidering a lot of Confucian Proverbs. There are also rooms for monks in the temple according to the level of monastic distribution.

大雄寶殿

Drawn by T. Allom.

Engraved by A. Willmore.

Great Temple at Honan Canton.

Le grand temple à Honan, Canton.

Grosser Tempel zu Honan, nahe Canton.

40 肇庆府的峡山

Xia Shan, Zhaoqing

广东肇庆府以东十英里，是最著名的西江关口，三条河流汇聚于此，形成一条商业水道，透过这条水道，人们得以和广州通商。以欧洲人的视野，这个峡山地区风景秀丽，犹如莱茵河。两岸矿藏丰饶，有银矿、锡矿、铁矿、金矿、宝石矿、煤矿和铜矿。其中宝石经过研磨，可以卖出高价。除了矿产，也有各种热带水果，产量丰富，还有黄花梨和铁木。英格兰人非常喜欢的孔雀也是峡山土生土长的动物。

画中左下角，有居民常住水上，粗糙木筏就是水上村庄的安身之地。这些居民大多是运输当地矿产或木材到广州的人。

10 miles east of Zhaoqing is the most famous Xi-jiang Crossing, where three rivers gather here, forming a commercial waterway. Through this waterway, people can trade with Guangzhou. From the perspective of the European, this gap hill area has a beautiful scenery, like Rhine. Both sides of the river have rich minerals, including silver, tin, iron and coal, and even gold, mercury, gem, pewter and copper. The gem can be sold at a high price after being grinded. Besides minerals, there are various tropical fruits with rich output, rose wood and ironwood. The peacock the English likes very much is also the indigenous animal in the Gap Hill.

The left corner of the painting illustrates that some residents live on the water and rough rafts are necessary for the water village. Most of these residents are those transporting local minerals or timber to Guangzhou.

Drawn by T. Allom.

Engraved by E. Brandard.

The Hëa hills, Chaou-king-foo.

Hauteurs de Chaou-king-foo.

Die Hëa Berge, Chaou-king-foo.

韶州广岩寺

Guangyan Temple in Shaozhou

　　韶州境内的北江穿过广东，越过梅岭，在八百多英尺高的峭壁脚下冲出一个缺口。在这个著名的峡口和石柱群以北就是潮州城，城墙由砖石砌成。离城墙不远处就是河道的启航处，带有衬垫的平底船在这里换成轻巧、可供食宿的舢板。顺流而下，远远就能见到河面上凸起一道七百英尺高的悬崖，崖顶呈柱状，这里叫作广岩。悬空的岩石由灰黑色石灰石构成，岩脚下是一块宽阔平台，只高出水面几英尺，一条容易攀登的长长阶梯连接通往山里的佛寺。佛寺里有房间、地下室和壁龛，是僧侣修道苦行之地。

　　The North River in the territory of Shaozhou runs across Guangdong and Meiling, rushing a gap at the foot of an over 800 feet high cliff. The north of this famous gap and pillars is Chaozhou, whose city wall is made of bricks. Not far from the wall is the sailing of the river. Padded punts are changed into light sampans with accommodation. Down the river, a 700 feet high cliff bulging the river can be seen from far away. The top of the cliff is in the shape of pillar, called as the Wide Rock. Rocks hanging in the air are made of grey and black limestones. At the foot of the rock is a wide platform, higher than the water level a few feet. A long ladder easy to climb connects to the temple in the mountain. Rooms, kitchens, basements and niches made of stones are ascetic places for monks.

Drawn by T. Allom.

Engraved by C. T. Dixon.

Temple of the Bonzes in the Quang Yen Rock.

Le Temple des Bonzes, dans le rocher de Quang Yen.   *Tempel der Bonzes in dem Quang Yen Felsen.*

42 从香山要塞远眺澳门

Overlooking Macau from the Xiang-shan Fortress

坐落于半岛之上的澳门，长三英里，宽一英里，一侧是美丽弯曲的海湾，另一侧向海突出。在岩石隆起的山脊，倾斜的山坡上，教堂、修道院和角楼分布其中。一座狭窄的砂质地峡将半岛与广东香山连接起来。

香山这头，山顶上修建了要塞，一道有城垛的围墙分隔了基督徒和佛教徒，主事的清朝官员长驻澳门，管辖澳门当地的葡萄牙人，没有得到许可，违反规则都要受罚。葡萄牙在澳门的行政官员包括一位军事总督、一位法官和一位主教，每人年薪六百英镑。有约三万名华人居住在澳门，但他们只受中国当局管辖。

Located on the top of the peninsula, Macau is 3 miles long and 1 mile wide, with one side of beautiful bend of the bay and the other side of bulging towards the sea. On the ridge with the uplifting rocks and the sloping hillside, churches, monasteries and turrets are scattered. A narrow sandy isthmus connects the peninsula to Xiangshan in Guangdong.

On this side of Xiangshan, the fortress was built on the peak and the wall with battlements separated the Christian from the Buddhist. The principal officer was stationed in Macau for the long period, administrating the local Portuguese in Macau, who would be punished without observing the regulation and without permission. The executive officers from Portugal in Macau included one military governor, one judge and one bishop, with an annual salary of 600 pounds. There are about 30,000 Chinese living in Macau, administrated only by the Chinese authorities.

Engraved by S. Fisher.

Macao, from the Forts of Heang-shan.

Macao près des forts de Heang-shan.   Macao von der Festung Heang-shan.

太平昭关

Taiping Zhao Pass

昭关在安徽和州含山县，最有名的典故是春秋时期伍子胥过昭关，一夜白了头的故事。他奇迹般地逃出重重陷阱，带着夫差抵达吴国，最后夫差登上王位，任命伍子胥为统兵将领，率兵攻入楚国，为自己父兄报仇。

昭关位于太平府，在江南的繁华城市中，政治的重要性排名第十二，但若以如画的景色和精致的文明生活而论，太平府是江南第一。这里气候温和，土壤肥沃，水果蔬菜产量丰足，手工艺品质量佳。三条通航的河流汇聚，吸引制造商和营运商聚集于此，官府便在此设立昭关。

Zhao Pass is located in Hanshan County, He State, Anhui Province. The most famous allusion is: During the Spring and Autumn Period, Wu Zixu passed the Zhao pass, with hair becoming white overnight. He miraculously escaped heavy traps and arrived in Wu (a state during this period) with Fu Chai. Eventually, Fu Chai came to his throne and appointed Wu Zixu as the general commander, leading soldiers to Chu (a state during this period) and revenging for his father and brother.

Zhao Pass is located in Taiping Mansion in the prosperous city in Jiangnan. Although the political importance of it ranks the twelfth, its beautiful scenery and delicate civilized life can rank the first. Taiping Mansion has a mild climate, fertile soil, abundant vegetables and fruits and handicrafts with the best quality. Three navigable rivers converge here, attracting manufacturers and operators to gather here. Therefore, the government set up Zhao Pass here.

Drawn by T. Allom.

Engraved by J. Sands.

The Tae-ping Shaou Kwan.

Le Tae-ping, à Shaou Kwan.

Der Tae-ping Shaou Kwan.

妈阁庙

A-ma Temple

　　走进妈阁庙，见过庙内举行的宗教仪式，看到僧人穿着的服饰，以及实际生活的方式，欧洲人会情不自禁认为，比起其他中国寺庙，妈阁庙更接近基督教的修道院。

　　寺庙主殿正面是一个巨大的圆门，正对圆门是一个高高的祭坛，阳光就照映在神像上。僧人的工作是陪着许愿的香客，卖给他们红色的纸签，上面写着经文或香客向菩萨许愿的内容。顺着楼梯进到一个更小的广场，靠海那边的石栏杆雕刻着警句箴言，再往前出现一座小庙，里面供着一尊神像，神像上悬挂着大灯笼。

　　The European cannot help but believe that A-ma Temple is closer to the monastery of Christianity than other Chinese temples after entering A-ma Temple and seeing religious rituals, costumes where monks wear and their actual lifestyles.

　　The front side of the main hall is a huge round door, in front of which is a high altar. The sun exactly shines on the image of the god. The work of monks is to accompany pilgrims and sell them red paper, on which is the content of wishes by pilgrims or scriptures. Along stairs into a smaller square, on the stone railing by the side of the sea is carved with aphorisms. Then a small temple appears, where there is a statue of the God and big lanterns are hung on it.

Chapel in the great Temple, Macao.

Chapelle du grand Temple de Macao.

Kapelle in dem großen Tempel, Macao.

鼓浪屿

Gulangyu Island

　　厦门附近海域辽阔，可停泊数千艘船，水深也可容最大的船停泊海岸，是个适合航行的安全之地。但大清帝国将贸易移转至广州，因此，这里只见中国船只停泊。

　　鼓浪屿是这座城市的天然屏障，为厦门阻挡风浪。岛屿两侧各有一条水道通向隐约可见的海湾，入口处有几处岩石阻挡着朝内河奔驰而来的海水。在花岗岩的顶端修建了军事工程，看起来更加巍峨。岩石之间，可见气势恢宏的佛寺和宝塔，以及美轮美奂的私家庭园。然而，挡得了风浪，挡不了海盗，海湾内停泊的驳船船员必须严阵以待，随时抵御可能的袭击。

　　Xiamen, near the vast sea, can be the shelter for thousands of ships. The depth of water can even hold the largest ship to berth. It is a safe place for navigation, but the Qing Empire transferred the trade to Guang-zhou and only Chinese ships parked here.

　　Gulangyu Island is the natural barrier of this city, preventing wind and waves for Xiamen. There was a waterway leading to the gulf which was vaguely visi-ble. At the entrance were several rocks blocking the sea running towards the inner river. The military work was built on the top of the granite of the strait and suburbs, seeming even more towering. Among rocks, we can see magnificent and gallant temples and pagodas as well as sumptuous private gardens. However, it can block wind and waves, but it can't prevent pirates. The crew berth-ing in the harbor must be vigilant at any time to resist possible attacks.

Drawn by T. Allom.

Engraved by A. Le Petit.

Amoy, from the Outer Anchorage.

Amoy, vue prise du mouillage extérieur.

Amoy, von der Aussenseite des Hafens betrachtet.

厦门城门牌楼

Entrance into the City of Xiamen

对于往来经商的外国人士来说，厦门是个自由良港，是个友善的城市，这里的居民可能个个都是水手。早在 1842 年根据中英《南京条约》签定五口通商之前，1685 年迪莱特号商船曾开到厦门，1744年哈德威克号紧跟在后，1832 年阿莫斯特号也航行到了这里。但碍于清政府的政策，禁止与外国人通商，阻碍了厦门这个城市的商业发展。

牌楼的大门巨大厚重，但并不宏伟华丽，上面雕刻着龙，镌刻着孔子的箴言。最高点的船型尖顶支撑着两条鱼，象征厦门沿岸的深海渔业非常发达，百姓以海为生。

As for foreign foreigners, Xiamen is a free port and a friendly city. Residents here are all sailors. Before five trade ports were signed according to the Sino-British Treaty of Nanjing in 1842, the Di Leite merchant ship sailed to Xiamen in 1685, then Hardwick followed closely after it in 1744 and in 1832 Amos also arrived here. But owing to the policy in Qing Dynasty that it prevented Chinese from trading with foreigners and moved away the British factory, thus blocking the trade spirit of this city.

The gate is huge and thick instead of magnificent and gorgeous, carved with dragons and proverbs by Confucius. The top of the gate is like the steeple of the ship supporting two fish, symbolizing the prosperity of coastal deep-sea fish industry in Xiamen and people can't live without the sea.

Drawn by T. Allan.　　　　From a sketch on the spot by Lieut. White, Royal Marines.　　　　Engraved by S. Fisher.

Entrance into the City of Amoy.

Entrée de la ville d'Amoy.　　　　*Eingang zur Stadt Amoy.*

47 贾梅士洞

Jardim deliuse de Camoes Cave

　　位于澳门白鸽巢公园，亦称贾梅士公园，公园中有一石洞曰贾梅士洞。贾梅士是葡萄牙一个家喻户晓的诗人，他因触犯宫廷官员，被流放到澳门，隐居此洞，并在此处创作了葡萄牙著名的史诗《葡国魂》，字里行间流露出他的爱国情感。1849 年，马葵士在巴黎定制了一尊贾梅士的半身铜像置于洞中，并将洞构筑成葡萄牙风格的门拱，洞前石壁上还嵌有黑色大理石，上面用中葡两种文字镌书："才德超人，因妒被难；奇诗大兴，立碑传世。"贾梅士洞耸立在悬崖边，俯瞰着大海和群山。

　　Camoes Park is situated in the White Crane Net Park in Macao. In the park there is a cave named Camoes Cave. Camoes was a poet known by every household, and he was exiled to Macao due to offending high officials. He lived in seclusion in the cave and create a poem <Portuguese Soul> revealing his patriotic emotion. In 1849, Marque manufactured Camoes statue bust and settled it in the cave. The cave was later reconstructed into a kind of archway in Portuguese style, and there also elected a black marble stone with words in both Chinese and Portuguese languages reading as: A man of extreme talent and virtue,Been envied causing calamity, Rare poetry known by all people, Set up stone showing history. Camoes Cave stands on the high cliff, and overlooks the vast sea and mountains.

Drawn by T. Allom.

Engraved by S. Bradshaw.

The Grotto of Camoens, Macao.

La grotte du Camoens, a Macao.

Die Grotte von Camoens, Macao.

48 澳门妈阁庙前

In front of A-ma Temple in Macau

妈阁庙位于澳门的西南方,枕山临海,倚崖而建,周围古木参天,风光绮丽。主要建筑有大殿、弘仁殿、观音阁等殿堂。庙内主要供奉道教女仙妈祖。庙前明显的标志是两根高高的旗杆,旗杆顶以皇家标准在正方形的框架中装点三个明显的金球,还有三块石头纪念碑,上面刻有名字、头衔、颂词和祈祷文。妈阁庙前,官员、士兵、信徒、水手、乞丐、变戏法和卖唱者来来往往。矮墙上有一道栅栏,用窗花格装饰,并用乐器、画具、武器等点缀,诉说着一个连续的故事。

A-ma Temple is located half a mile away from the northwest of Macau. Two high flagpoles are obvious signs in front of the temple. On the top, there are three obvious gold balls decorated in the square frame according to the royal standard. There are three stone monuments, engraved with names, titles, eulogies and prayers. In front of A-ma Temple, soldiers, believers, sailors, beggars, jugglers and singers come back and forth. A fence on the low wall is decorated with grilles and dotted with musical instruments, paintings and weapons, in order to tell a series of stories.

Engraved by S. Bradshaw.

Façade of the Great Temple at Macao.

Façade du grand Temple à Macao.   Vorderseite des großen Tempels zu Macao.

49 香港的竹渠

Bamboo Canal in Hong Kong

　　住在面积狭小、地势起伏的香港，当地居民总能充分发挥因地制宜、就地取材的能力，增加每一分地的产能。此画风景为女王城后方的乡间，幽谷纵横，平地宽阔，巨石林立，稻田的周围有峭壁拔地而起，形成鲜明对比。香港鼓励人们在峡谷中种植树木，峡谷之中村庄错落，树荫供人们避开狠毒的阳光。为了将贫瘠土壤变为良田，居民发明竹渠，将水引出峡谷，灌溉远处干旱的平原。将竹竿钻孔后即可导水，竹子结实的部分可作为一根根的桩，围起来成为篱笆，或作为轿子的轿杆。

　　Living in Hong Kong with a narrow size and rolling terrain, the local residents could always make use of conditions and increase the productive ability of every field. This painting is the countryside behind the Queen City, where valleys are perpendicular and horizontal, the flat is wide and huge stones stand in great numbers. Around the rice field are cliffs springing up, making a sharp contrast. The Hong Kong government encouraged people to plant trees in the valley. Villages are scattered in the valley and the shade can protect people from vicious sunshine. In order to turn the barren soil into the fertile land, residents invent the bamboo drainage to lead water out of the valley and water the arid plain far away. Making holes in the bamboo pole can guide water. What's more, the solid part of the bamboo can be served as root piles. They can be surrounded as a fence or the pole to support a sedan chair.

Engraved by H. Adlard.

Bamboo Aqueduct, at Hong Kong.

Aquéduc de Bambou à Hong Kong.   *Bambus Waßerleitung zu Hong Kong.*

50 小布达拉宫

The Little Potala Palace

每年夏天，清朝的皇帝总是要到热河郊外避暑，尽管路途遥远，但沿途每隔一段距离，就到行宫休憩，趁此机会探访各地世袭的领地，接见在天威之下的大小可汗，以巩固自己的疆域。空闲时狩猎或到大禅寺里祈祷，奉献供品。

画中的宫殿和花园，就位于大河边的山谷里，紧邻热河小镇。这里群山环绕，崎岖险峻，皇帝陛下在护卫的陪同下，走向小布达拉宫。这座建筑呈正方形，每边长二百英尺，主建筑物楼高十一层，正面墙壁上的十一排窗户最引人注目。

The emperor in Qing Dynasty always goes to the summer resort in the suburb of Jehol every summer. Despite the long way, there is a palace for rest after a specific distance. The emperor can take advantage of this opportunity to visit the hereditary territory in the country and Khans governed by him to consolidate his domain. During the free time, the emperor will hunt and devote offerings so as to pray in the Great Temple.

The palace and garden in the painting are located in the valley near the river, close to the hot river town surrounded by mountains. Owing to the rugged road, the emperor goes to the little Potala Palace with the company of guards. The building is square and 200 feet long. The main building is 11 stories tall and the 11 rows of windows on the front wall are in the spotlight.

Drawn by T. Allom.

Engraved by J. Tingle.

The Poo-ta-la, or Great Temple near Zhehol, Tartary.

Le Poo-ta-la, ou le grand Temple, près de Zhehol. Tartarie.

Der Poo-ta-la, oder grosse Tempel, bei Zhehol. Tartarei.

51 迎亲队伍

The Welcoming Team of the Wedding

婚礼当天，新郎的父亲为新郎戴上头冠。新娘在出发前，将头发梳成发髻，再由同伴帮她修面，之后陪着她哭泣，等待离家时刻的到来。

迎亲队伍带着各种家用品，包括衣服、被褥和其他贵重的物品。衣服就装在雕花木箱里，家禽和猪也带着，象征忠贞和夫妻关系的鹅也在队伍中。旗手扛着旗子，吹鼓手吹着唢 、敲着鼓，迎亲队伍一路唱着歌。新娘坐在布满了大红色和金色的花轿里，那亮眼的颜色提醒着世人，这位女性具有美貌与美德。连站在花轿后面的仆人，也穿着大红色的制服，长辈则坐着轿子，一路跟在新娘的花轿后面。

On the wedding day, the groom's father put on the crown for him: a cloth cap first, and then a leather cap, at last a corolla. Before the bride sets out, her hair will be combed into a bun and her face will be shaved by her companions. At last, companions will cry with her and it's time to wait for leaving home.

The welcoming team carries a various household items including clothes, beddings and other precious items. Clothes will be in the carved wooden case. Even poultries and pigs are carried, with geese symbolizing chastity and loyalty. Standard-bearers are shouldering the flags, trumpeters are blowing suona horns (a Chinese traditional musical instrument like the trumpet), drummers are beating drums and the welcoming team is singing all the way. The bride sits inside the flower sedan padded with red and golden colours. These bright colours are meant to signify that the bride is a lady with beauty both outside and inside (virtue). Even the servants standing behind the sedan are in red. The elderly in the family also sit in the sedan, following the flower sedan of the bride.

Drawn by T. Allom. Engraved by S. Bradshaw.

Chinese Marriage Procession.

Procession de mariage. Feierlicher Aufzug bei einer Trauung.

收受聘礼

Acceptance of Betrothal Presents

传统的中国婚礼从收受聘礼那一刻算起，而且聘礼与嫁妆成正比。

画中下聘的仪式显得隆重，女方家人一脸严肃地接待来下聘的人，周围环坐新娘的姐妹和直系亲属。头戴绣花帽的新娘站在显眼的地方，向宾客表达谢意。包括饰品、卫生用具、绸缎和银制品等聘礼，由家中年长女性先收起来，再交由新娘父母保管。由于聘礼品项多，下聘仪式前，新娘家里还必须腾出房间作为收受聘礼之用。

The traditional Chinese wedding begins with the acceptance of betrothal presents, which are in proportion to the dowry.

In the painting, the ceremony of sending betrothal presents seems grand. The bride's family treat seriously, with sisters and family members sitting around. The bride wearing an embroidered hat stands in a conspicuous place to express her gratitude to guests. Presents include jewelries, sanitary wares, silk and silver products and so on. They are accepted by the older female in the family first, and then they will be reserved by the bride's parents. Owing to a great number of presents, the bride's family have to make room for acceptance in advance.

Drawn by T. Allom. Engraved by W. Floyd.

Arrival of Marriage Presents at the bridal residence.

Arrivée des présents de noces à la demeure de la fiancée. *Ankunft der Hochzeit-Geschenke in der Wohnung der Braut.*

53 中国商人的园林

Gardens of Chinese Businessmen

　　从欧洲人的视野看中国的园林，复杂而浑然一体的格局难以模仿，除非亲自到中国实地旅游勘察。凿湖造地，砌石成山，小桥流水，假山池沼，或与水相邻，或始于花圃，园林的奇思妙想让外国人啧啧称奇。

　　宅邸的设计也与西方国家不同，中国南方宅邸的特色是有阳台遮阳，支撑房间的椽梁，材质往往是松木，常见彩漆无纹，但也有刻意雕刻过。椽木上覆盖着凹状的琉璃瓦，看起来很像英格兰的屋面瓦，青砖黛瓦视觉效果好。屋顶是最花心思的，两侧的山墙装点着金龙和云彩的图案，有的则装点天上飞鸟和林中野兽等图案。

From the perspective of the European, Chinese gardens are complicated and hard to imitate because of their seamless patterns except the tourism exploration about China. The abundant and interesting imagination of gardens amaze foreigners with chiseling lake and land, laying stones into mountains, bridges and flowing water and rockery ponds. Gardens are either near water or in the flower nursery from the start point.

The design of the mansion is also different from that in western countries. The feature of the mansion in the south of China has a balcony shade. In order to support rafters of the room, the quality tends to be pine and the most common style is colour paint without grain. There is also a style engraved deliberately. Rafters are covered with concave glazed tiles, like the roof tile in England. Green bricks with white seam have a good visual effect. The roof takes the most time to think and both sides of the upper part of the sharp mountain are decorated with gold dragons and the pattern of clouds. Others are decorated with birds in the sky, beasts in the forest and other patterns.

House of a Chinese Merchant, near Canton.

From a Drawing in the possession of Sir Geo. Staunton, Bart:

Maison d'un marchand chinois près de Canton.   Haus eines chinesischen Kaufmanns bei Canton.

54 丽泉行潘长耀别墅

The Villa of Liquan Firm Pan Chang-yao

位于广州近郊，丽泉行商人潘长耀的别墅，比起清朝一些官员的宅邸，更为富丽堂皇。这位在中国历史上第一位为生意打国际官司的商人，兴建别墅也不遗余力。在浓荫遮蔽的园林中，廊柱、阳台、飞檐和垂柳抵御着阳光日晒，湖水带来了清凉舒适。雕梁画栋的楼房，显得金碧辉煌，门廊上以倒置的莲花点缀，连游船的船身也装饰得很有艺术感。船上的贵妇名媛一身绸缎旗袍，她们日常生活的行动范围常常仅限于走过小桥，从露台到凉亭，再从凉亭到宝塔。

Located in the outskirt of Guangzhou, the villa of businessman Pan Changyao of Liquan Firm was even more luxurious than official residences. This businessman was the one who is the first businessman to engage in an international lawsuit for his career. He spared no effort to construct the villa. In the garden with thick shades, pillars, balconies, cornices and weeping willows prevent the sunshine and the lake brings cool and comfortable feeling. In buildings with carved beams, beams and pillars are coated with a layer of gold. The porch is dotted with the lotus inversed and even bodies of boats are decorated in an art way. As for ladies in satin cheongsams on board, their daily activities are limited to walking cross the small bridge, from the terrace to the pavilion and then from the pavilion to the pagoda.

Drawn by T. Allom.

Engraved by C. T. Dixon.

The Fountain-Court in Conseequas House, Canton.

(From a drawing in the possession of Sir G. Staunton, Bart.)

La cour de la fontaine dans la maison de Conseequa, à Canton.

Das Brunnenzimmer in Conseequa's Haus, Canton.

天津大剧院

马可·波罗如此描述天津：位于京杭大运河进入北京河段的位置，负责北直隶省（管辖河北、北京、天津）和山东省沿海盐运的清朝高官驻扎于此，所有从东北地区运木材的船只，通过辽东湾之后，都要在此卸除。

当时的英国人则以"中国利物浦"来形容这个熙来攘往的商业城市。抵达此地的人们，不必担心没有休闲去处，到处都有娱乐公演、咖啡厅、餐馆、礼堂和剧院里客人络绎不绝。白河岸边停船的码头永远挤满了人，人流沿着堤岸从房屋走向水边，两岸缓慢下降的地势让这里看起来就像个圆形大剧场。

The Tianjin Grand Theatre

Marco Polo once described Tianjin like this: Tianjin is located in the Beijing-Hangzhou Grand Canal into the section of the river in Beijing, where senior officials who take the responsibility of the coastal salt transport in the northern Zhili Province (Hebei, Beijing and Tianjin) and Shandong Province are stationed. Many vessels transporting wood from the northeast region will unload it after passing across Liaodong Bay.

British at that time described this bustling commercial city as "Liverpool in China". People arriving here are not necessary to worry about no places to go. Everywhere is crowded with entertaining performances and guests, including cafes, restaurants, auditoriums and theatres. The wharf of the river bank is always filled with people. They walk along from the slope of the house to the river. The slow decline of terrain makes it look like a round theatre.

Drawn by T. Allom.

Engraved by R. Sands.

Theatre at Tien-Sin.

Théâtre à Tien-Sin.

Theater zu Tien-Sin.

野台戏

The Outdoor Traditional Drama

　　过去中国对于民间戏剧表演团体并不重视，演员大多过着漂泊的生活，一边表演，一边流浪于乡镇之间。到了某个定点，剧团会立起一个离地八英尺高的舞台，用多根木桩支撑着弧形屋檐，自由入座的观众从三面可以清楚地看到舞台。舞台对面设置独立的包厢，供权贵和付钱的观众看戏。方方正正的包厢里，前厅的座位是贵妇与千金小姐专用，其他座位则给男宾客，招待清朝官员的，除了点心，还有烟管。戏台下通常站有管事的衙役，如果有人推挤，这些衙役便会严惩闯入者。当时有一出名为《日月奇观》的戏很受欢迎，此画便是演出过程中的一幕景象。

　　In the past, China did not pay much attention to the folk drama performance. Most of these performers live a wandering life: perform and wander between all kinds of townships. At a certain point, the troupe will set up a stage 9 feet high, supporting the curved eave with many stakes. The audience can be free seated and look at the stage from three sides clearly. Opposite the stage is independent boxes for the expensive and the audience paying to watch the play. In the square box, seats in front are dedicated to rich ladies and their daughters. Other seats are left for male guests. Snacks as well as smoking pipes will be prepared to serve Qing officers. Under the stage is often stationed runners in order to punish intruders if someone wants to break in. At that time, the most popular drama was called "Sun and Moon Wonders". This painting is one scene taken from the performing process.

Drawn by T. Allom.

Engraved by R. Staines.

Scene from the Spectacle of "The Sun and Moon."

Spectacle du Soleil et de la Lune.

Scene im Schauspiel "Die Sonne und der Mond."

57 二月初二迎春赛会

每年农历二月初二，是土地公的生日，中国南方举行迎春赛会，其中水牛节和人庆节最为隆重。

举行水牛节时，游行队伍浩浩荡荡朝着土地公庙前进，队伍中，男孩子打扮成羊怪或农神，坐在粗糙的祭坛或树枝上，由轿子抬着走来；小女孩打扮成山茶花的模样，象征茶叶的实用性和鲜花盛开之美，还有一群穿着彩衣的壮汉抬着一头黏土制作的水牛。到了寺庙门口，前一天已等候在那里的道长迎上前去，担任春分祭祀的主祭，只见他身穿刺绣精美的华服，站在伞盖下向众人发表演说。至于人庆节的游行状况则和水牛节差不多。

The Spring Festival Competition on the Second Day of February

The second day of February according to the lunar calendar every year is the birthday of the Village Deity. In the south of China, the Spring Festival Competition is held, among which Buffalo Festival and Man-day are the most solemn celebrations.

When holding Buffalo Festival, the parade moves towards the God of the Earth on a large scale. Among the parade, boys were dressed as sheep monsters or agricultural god, sitting on rough altars or branches, carried from sedans; Girls were dressed as camellia, symbolizing the utility of tea and the beauty of blooming flowers; A group of strong people in colour lifted up the buffalo made of clay. At the entrance of the temple, the master waiting there a day ago came in front and served as the spring deacon monk. Wearing the exquisite embroidered costume, he was addressing the lecture under the umbrella. As for Man-day, the situation is similar.

Drawn by T. Allom.

Engraved by S. Bradshaw.

Ceremony of "Meeting the Spring."

Chinois allant en cérémonie saluer la venue du printemps.

Chinesen gehen dem Frühling entgegen.

58 元宵灯节

The Lantern Festival

19 世纪的中国，在一年的众多节日里，最华丽的当属元宵节。每年到了这一天，民众可以停工四十天，参加由富人出钱、穷人出力的活动盛会——灯笼和烟火艺术展。

无论是屋檐、角楼、寺庙、大桥或船上，都装饰着形状各异、材质不一的灯笼。许多人提着灯笼排着长队去庙里拜神，有的灯笼像发光的鱼，口里还会吐出火焰，还有中国人最爱的龙形灯笼，眼睛不时喷火，其他飞鸟、游鱼和动物形状的灯笼全部汇聚一堂，在空中游曳。此外，燃放各式烟花炮竹，烟火表演也是重头戏。

There is no doubt that the most gorgeous festival among festivals in one year is the Lantern Festival in the 19th century in China. On this day every year, the populace can stop working for forty years, participating in the grandiose activity supported by the rich and the poor——the art exhibition of lanterns and fireworks.

Whether eaves, turrets, temples, bridges or boats are all decorated with lanterns in different shapes and materials. Many people carry lanterns, lining up to pray in the temple. Some lanterns are like shiny fish, with the mouth spitting out the flame. Chinese favorite dragon-shaped lanterns can make fire from their eyes. Other lanterns in the shape of birds and fish all assemble and swim in the air. In addition, the firework show like setting off fireworks is a main event during the festival.

THE IMPERIAL GARDENS

im Nanking in China

Philadelphia: N. A. Bibliographic Institution

端午龙舟赛

The Boat Race on Dragon Boat Festival

麒麟、玄武、凤凰和龙四种神兽，是中国文化重要的象征。相传麒麟主管文学，会在圣人降生时出现；玄武主管美德，在德行普及与和平时刻现身；凤凰象征祥瑞，若天下盛世，凤凰飞来；龙则象征权威，各种戒律、文件、书籍、皇朝的仪器均用龙为标志。

然而，中国人认为龙会吞食太阳和月亮，让人间笼罩黑暗，为了平息龙的愤怒，转移龙的注意力，每年农历五月五日别会举行龙舟大赛。19 世纪的赛龙舟，船中央摆放牛皮大鼓，三名鼓手奋力敲击，一名小丑随着大鼓的节奏表演，船头甲板上的两个人挥舞尖戟，大声吼叫。

Four mythical creatures including Kirin, Basaltic, phoenix and dragon are the most important symbols in China. Kirin is said to be responsible for literature, which will appear until the birth of sages. Basaltic is responsible for virtue, which will appear until the virtue and peace spread throughout the whole world. Phoenix symbolizes an auspicious sign. If the world is peaceful and prosperous, the phoenix will come. Dragon symbolizes authority, which can be applied into all kinds of rules, documentaries, books and royal instruments.

However, it is universally acknowledged by Chinese that the dragon will swallow the sun and the moon, covering the world with darkness. In order to ease the dragon's fury and shift its attention, the dragon boat race is held on May 5 according to the lunar calendar every year. In the 19th century, the race was such a picture: in the centre of the boat was a big leather drum, with three drum players beating with all the strength. A clown performed with the rhythm of drums. Two people on the deck were waving halberd and shouting loudly.

Drawn by T. Allom.

Engraved by R. Brandard.

Festival of the Dragon-Boat, 5th day of 5th Moon.

七月普渡

Mid-summer Ghost Festival in July

佛教故事里目犍连亲赴阎王殿救回自己的母亲，分享了他在阴间的见闻：贤能者得到福报，恶人则受到惩罚。他吩咐人们，应该准备祭品祭祀亲友的阴魂。随着故事的流传，每年农历七月一日开始，信奉佛教的人们到佛殿或寺庙，甚至自己搭建临时的灵棚祭祖祀亲。当时祭祀的现场，墙上会悬挂着恶人被押解到阴曹地府受审，周围站着牛头马面的图画，以警示人们。出家法师在旁指导仪式，为亡者唱诵梵呗，祭祀的人们准备各种美味食物和冥纸，冥纸代表钱财，以及各种纸扎用品。仪式结束，食物奉献给僧人，冥纸和纸扎则送进香炉焚烧。

The bullock mujianlian went to the hell to save his mother on his own and shared the knowledge that the virtuous could be blessed, while the wicked could be punished. What's more, he commanded that people should prepare oblations for their dead relatives and friends. With the spread of the story, those who believe in Buddhism goes to the Buddha hall, the temple and even their own temporary funeral sheds for ancestor worship every year beginning with July 1 according to the lunar calendar. At that time, on the wall will hang the scene that the wicked are arrested to the hell to be punished with devils in animal forms around in order to alert people. The ascetic master will guide the ceremony beside and sing the chanting for the dead. People will prepare for all kinds of delicious food, joss paper representing fortune and all kinds of paper supplies. After the ceremony, food will be devoted to monks and these joss paper will be burnt in the incense burner.

Drawn by T. Allom.   Engraved by E. Challis.

Propitiatory Offerings for departed Relatives.

Offrandes propitiatoires pour des parents morts.   Versöhnungsopfer für hingeschiedene Verwandte.

61 中秋祭拜

The Worship during the Mid-Autumn Festival

这是在距离扬州城几里之遥的一个小城镇里，远望可以看到一座耸立着的高塔，后面的稻田正准备栽种第二季作物。农家在中秋节当天，带着家人祭拜谷神和土地公，感恩过去一年神明的照应，祈求团圆、幸福吉祥。让外国人感到惊讶的是，画面中一家人在祭坛前跪拜用的垫子、一家之主戴的帽子、柱廊下的桌子和神龛，全部都用树干、藤条或麻绳做成。甚至连后方的棚屋、大门和晒谷场的篱笆、谷筛都是以藤条为材料。

In a small town, a few miles away from Yangzhou, the tall tower can be seen from a far distance. The paddy field behind is being prepared for planting crops for the second season. On the Mid-Autumn Festival, farmers will bring the whole family to worship the Valley God and the Village Deity to express gratitude for the care of the god. To foreigners' surprise, mats for the family before the altar, the hat for the host of the family and the table and the shrine under the colonnade will all be made of tree trunks, rattans or hemps. Even the rear of the shed, the gate, the fence and the griddle of the farm are made by the rattan.

Drawn by T. Allom.

Engraved by Aug.ᵗ Fox.

Chinese Sacrifice to the Harvest Moon.

Sacrifice du Chung-tsue-Tsee, ou lune de la moisson.   *Opfer des Chung-tsue-Tsee, oder Herbstfier.*

重阳放风筝

Flying Kites on the Double Ninth Festival

"九月九，风吹（风筝）满天啸"。重阳节放风筝是重要的中国民俗。明清时期，放风筝以京城、山东潍坊、江苏南通和直隶天津四个地方最为有名。每年到了这一天，家里的长辈和小孩一起来到市郊的空旷处，享受着一整天放风筝的乐趣。当白天的活动将要结束时，民众会用风筝比高下，努力让彼此的风筝碰撞或让风筝线缠绕，以便扯断对方的风筝，不成功便让风筝随风吹走，意谓"衰运"尽去，"好运"将来。风筝的造型丰富，有猫头鹰、蜈蚣、鲤鱼等，个个栩栩如生，晴空下，远望犹如一群动物在嬉戏，非常壮观。

"September 9 is the day with kites blowing throughout all the sky." Flying kites is the most important Chinese custom. During Ming and Qing Dynasties, the capital city, Weifang in Shandong Province, Nantong in Jiangsu Province and Tianjin are most famous for this custom. On this day every year, the old and children go to the highest place of the suburb, enjoying flying kites all day long. When the daytime activity ends, the populace will compete with their kites by trying to make their kites run into each other, or winding the line so as to break lines of others. If they fail, they will let their kites fly away with wind, symbolizing bad luck goes and good luck comes. On account of abundant shapes of kites including owls, eagles, centipedes, carps and so on which are all lifelike, it's spectacular to see a crowd of animals playing in the sky from the far distance.

Drawn by T. Allom.   Engraved by A. Willmore.

Kite-flying at Hae-kwan, on the Ninth Day of Ninth Moon.

插秧

插秧，农村莳秧的一种方法，又叫插田。一般秧苗长到 3−5 寸长时即可移栽，即叫插秧。第一天插秧，称为"开秧门"。主妇要备好饭菜酒肉，供家人和帮工者聚餐。餐间，每人要吃一个鸡蛋，意谓"讨彩头"。蹲下去拔秧，先用缚秧苗的稻草在秧田上面横扫几下，意谓防止"发秧疯"。发秧疯即手背发肿。插秧结束，称"关秧门"，有的户主绕田走一圈，拔一把秧苗带回家，扔在门墙边，说是"秧苗认得家门，丰收由此进门"。插秧结束那天的晚餐，主人家要宴请帮工者，称"打散"。插秧种田时，一天三餐外，还要加两次点心。

Transplant Rice Seedlings

Transplant rice seedlings wss a way farmers tending the rice seedlings. When the seedlings grew to 3-5 inches, farmers could transplant them. Farmers called the first day of the work as "open-door-transplanting".and one the day, housewife should prepare a rich meal and wine receiving laborers including family members and other helpers. Everyone should eat an egg which meant the work could go smoothly. At first,farmers should pull the seedling out, and before pulling, they always used a strew rope to wipe over the field, believing that could prevent them from suffering "seedling mad", a kind of disease of swelling hands. When the transplanting finished, the farmers would walk circling the field and brought a handful seedling back to threw them in front of the door, believing that the rice could know host's home, and promise a bumper harvest. On the day, the housewife should also made a rich supper for laborers, that they called "disperse supper". During the work, the housewife provided three meals adding two times of refreshment per day.

Drawn by T. Allom.

Engraved by T. A. Prior.

Transplanting Rice.

Transplantation du riz.

THE LONDON PRINTING AND PUBLISHING COMPANY, LIMITED

Verpflanzung des Reis.

64 苏州府播种水稻

Suzhou - Planting Rice

　　水稻偏爱潮湿土壤，易于栽种，每年可播种两次，画中为苏州府播种水稻的情形。自古以来，稻米即是人们的主粮，谈到有关"吃"的词汇里，吃饭、早饭、午饭、晚饭，少不了"饭"字。稻米由于生长速度快，营养价值虽不如小麦高，但含有少量的谷蛋白，物美价廉，非常适合作为穷苦阶层的营养品。

　　除了能够让人填饱肚子，水稻的其他用途也十分广泛，稻秆捣成浆状后可以制成各种人偶、雕像和盘子，等到变硬后，用彩纹加以装点。在棉花工厂里，纺工就是用它来为经线上浆的。

　　Rice prefers wet soil and is easy to plant, which can be planted twice every year. The painting is the situation that people in Suzhou mansion are planting rice. Rice has been the staple food for Chinese since the ancient time. When it comes to the Chinese dictionary about eating including eating, breakfast, lunch and dinner, one Chinese word is vital: (rice in Chinese). Owing to the fast growth rate, the nutrition in rice is not as much as that in wheat. But it has a little protein and is not expensive, suitable for the poor class. In addition to filling the stomach, there are a wide range of functions. When the straw turns into paste, it can be made into all kinds of figures, sculptures and pans. When it turns hard, we can decorate it with colorful strips. In the cotton factory, spinners make use of it for pasting the thread.

Drawn by T. Allom.

Engraved by W. Wetherhead.

Sowing Rice at Soo-chow-foo.
(Province of Kiang-si.)

Ensemencement du riz, à Soo-chow-foo.
(Province de Kiang-si.)

Reis Aussaat in Soo-chow-foo.
(Provinz Kiang-si.)

65

东昌府的米贩子

Rice traders of Dongchang Mansion

京杭大运河沿岸，常有专卖饭食的小摊子。在东昌府辖下的沿岸，为了征收盐税设置的岗亭，成了过往船只的歇脚之处。画面中监工在征税，警卫队来回巡逻。纤夫们聚集在用竹竿撑起的大伞之下，围坐在一个土灶前，有的脱下竹帽，将长辫子盘在头上；有的还来不及脱下帽子，便拿起碗筷，狼吞虎咽地吃了起来；还有的则在一旁抽起长烟斗来。靠近纤夫的地上，还放着穿着绳索的平板，这些平板纤夫在拉纤时可以置放胸口，以减缓纤绳过大的拉力。

Along Beijing-Hangzhou Grand Canal always sets the small stall selling food which is administrated by Dongchang Mansion. It becomes a specific post for imposing the salt tax as well as for slaves stopping ships to rest. Supervisors impose taxes, the police patrol back and forth and slaves gather together under the big umbrella supported by bamboo rods, sitting in front of a stove. Some took off their bamboo hats, with braids around heads. Others are too late to take off hats in order to devour food cooked by the hostess ravenously. Those slaves who haven't bought dishes yet are smoking with long pipes. On the ground near slaves are put flats with ropes, which can be placed on the chest to lessen the excessive pulling tension.

Rice Sellers at the Military Station of Tong-Chang-foo.

Drawn by T.Allom.

Engraved by R.Staines.

Marchandes de riz à la station militaire de Tong-Chang-foo.   *Reishändler in der Garnison zu Tong-Chang-foo.*

宁波的棉花种植

Cotton Growing in Ningbo

明清之际，江南地区的棉纺织业十分发达，长江三角洲地区是明清棉花种植和棉布纺织的主要地区。宁波三面环山，北部的平原靠海湾，多沙土，含盐碱，适宜种植棉花。

画面中描绘了农人在一片农作物田中劳动的情形。远处有个傍山的小城，城中竖立着一座塔，民居隐约可见，画面的背景是连绵的棉田和山丘。这幅有一片棉花田环绕的古城图画，还曾经出现在1928年中国工业发展银行（劝业银行）发行的两角面额纸币上。

The cotton textile industry had been very prosperous in Ming and Qing dynasties in Yangtze Delta, where was then the main area of cotton production. Ningbo was surrounded by mountains in three sides, and with a vast plain nearing the sae gulf, so the fields rich in sand, salt and alkali were fitting to grow cotton.

The painting described farmers working on the field. There was a town aside the mountain and a pagoda stood above the town. The people's residences were within sight, and the background of them were mountains, hill-slope and cotton fields. This painting had appeared on 0.2 yuan note issued by China Industry Development Bank in 1928.

Drawn by T. Allom.

Engraved by A. Le Petit.

Cotton Plantations at Ning-po.

Plantation de Coton à Ning-po.

Baumwolle Pflanzschule zu Ning-po.

茶艺茶文化

Tea Arts and Tea Culture

19 世纪的中国，江苏省和浙江省盛产绿茶，纬度较低的福建和江西两省则种植红茶，主要销往欧洲和美国。当时茶叶的品种由贸易商决定，据说起源于广东商人。当时的红茶品种有武夷茶、小种茶、清茶、开花香和橙白毫；绿茶品种有屯溪茶、熙春茶、嫩熙茶、皇家贡茶、珠茶，其中皇家贡茶又称"御茶"，只有在典礼上喝得到，或是进贡给皇帝。由于茶在当时非常流行，一位外国牧师就说："在商店和游客川流不息的地方，家家柜台上或茶几上都摆放着一把盛茶水的大茶壶，茶壶周围摆满了茶杯，这是为口渴的顾客准备的。"

In the 19th century in China, Jiangsu Province and Zhejiang Province are rich in green tea and Fujian Province and Jiangxi Province with low latitude are rich in black tea, main exporting to Europe and America. The type of the tea was decided by traders at that time, originating from businessmen in Guangdong Province. Black tea includes Wuyi tea, Kung Fu tea, Madai tea, souchong tea, green tea, blooming fragrance, orange pekoe;Green tea includes twankay (tea), hyson (tea) and royal tribute tea. The royal tribute tea is also known as "imperial tea", which can be drunk only at the ceremony or during the tribute to the emperor. As tea was very popular at that time, according to a foreign priest, "In some places like shops and where tourists visit, every shop will place a large tea pot on the counter or tea table, with cups around to prepare for thirsty customers."

Drawn by T. Allom.　　　　　　　　　　　　　Engraved by A.Willmore.

The culture and preparation of Tea.

Culture et Préparation du Thé.　　　　　　　Pflanzen und Zubereitung des Thee.

68 茶船装货

Tea Ship Loading

画中所绘是福建九曲河的支流上，一个以茶闻名的度假胜地，也是茶叶集散地。这里的山谷和丘陵适合出产茶叶，从种植到输出，连贯作业。

当茶苗长成茶树，三年内或长到四英尺高之前，不能做任何采集动作。同一棵茶树上，新长出的细叶子嫩芽就是小种茶，次之是功夫茶，再次之是福建武夷茶。

厂家将购得的茶叶运回工厂，然后进行挑选，按不同的品级归类，最后放进箱子里，用简便的形式将茶叶运到陈塘码头或其他茶船上，运往广东和澳门。

In the painting is the tributary of Jiuqu River in Fujian Province, which is a resort famous for tea and a tea centre. Valleys and hills here are suitable for producing teas from planting to output, in a consistent way.

When tea seeds grow into tea trees, they can't be picked before reaching the height of 4 feet within three years. On the same tea tree, the tender shoot growing small leaves is souchong tea followed by the kanboyi tea, Kung Fu tea and Wuyi Tea in Fujian Province according to the quality.

Manufacturers transport tea they have bought back to the factory, taking out of some tea from every level of tea and combining them into the level of tea they want. At last, the tea is put into box and transported to Chentang pier or other tea ships in the simplest way in order to ship to Guangdong Province and Macau.

Drawn by T. Allom.

Engraved by J. Tingle.

Loading Tea-junks at Tseen-tang.

Chargement des jonques à thé, à Tseen-tang.

Das Laden der Thee Böte zu Tseen-tang.

煮茧缫丝

Cooking Cocoon and Reeling Silk

　　桑蚕归类蛾属，土生土长于中国，昆虫学家称为"家蚕"，在发育的过程中，根据不同的种类，脱壳三四次后变成蛹，身上呈白色，等到上面有蓝色或黄色的斑点，便不用再喂食，蛹会努力化成蛾。蚕蛹化成蛾后，蚕会吐出黏黏的分泌物，附着在蚕蛹表面，慢慢形成卵状的球包裹着身体。大约经过十天的吐丝，就可以从蚕茧中抽取蚕丝，这一过程称为缫丝。

　　缫丝是一道工艺要求十分严格的工序，水质、水温及浸泡时间等因素都会影响蚕丝的品质。中国古人经过长期实践，总结出一整套行之有效的缫丝经验，中国也因此成为世界优质蚕丝的主要产地。

　　Silk worm which belongs to the category of moth, had originally grown in China, so the entomologists named it as household silk worm. On the process of growing, the worms could shed their shell for 3-4 times. When the worms turned into white and showed up blue or yellow dots on skin, the breeders stopped feeding them, and the worms began to spit secretion that turned out as cocoons encircling themselves. In the cocoons, and the warm transformed them as chrysalis. About more than 10 days, the chrysalis would become moth, and breeders must reel the cocoons before the moth appearing. The reeling silk was a fine craft, the temperature and quality of water should effect the quality of silk. Chinese ancestors had summed up a series of effective experience. China, therefore, had become the main area for producing good quality silk in history.

Drawn by T. Allom.

Engraved by J. Davies.

Destroying the Chrysalides and reeling the Cocoons.

Etouffement de la chrysalide et devidage du Cocon.

Zerstören der Raupen Puppen und Haspeln der Seide.

70 养蚕人家

The Sericulture Family

养蚕是古代中国人创造的重要技艺，种桑养蚕之法相传源于黄帝的妻子嫘祖。到了汉文帝年间，丝绸开始备受推崇，并被缝制成富人阶级最流行的裙子。在中国市场中，江南地区生产的丝绸最为昂贵。比起印度、土耳其或意大利的丝绸，英国商人更爱中国江南地区所产的丝绸。

由于养蚕缫丝的成本低，获利快，许多家庭的女性也纷纷投入这项工作。画面中的一家老小，不分男女，通通投入，忙着养蚕、整理蚕茧，犹如家庭工厂。养蚕的最重要食物是桑叶，中国种植的是白桑树，意大利生长的是黑桑树，美国则有红桑树。

In the past, people often wore woolen sweaters. During the Han Dynasty, silk which can be made into skirts began to be popular among the rich class. In the Guangdong market, Zhejiang and Jiangnan region produced the most expensive silk, doubling the price of the ordinary one. Compared with silk made in India, Turkey or Italy, British businessmen love Jiangnan silk more.

Due to the low cost and immediate profit of silkworm reeling, women in the family devoted to this work. In the painting, regardless of men, women, the old or the young, they are all busy feeding sericulture and finishing cocoon, like a family factory. Mulberry leaves are the most important food. China plants white mulberry trees, Italy plants black mulberry trees and the USA plants red mulberry trees.

Drawn by T. Allom.

Engraved by A. Willmore.

Feeding Silkworms, and Sorting the Cocoons.

Plantation des vers à soie et assortissement des Cocons.　　　　Füttern der Seidenwürme, und Sortirung der Puppen.

染丝坊

The Silk Dyeing Workshop

　　在一个两尺深的池塘，周围有一排房屋，这是用来进行漂洗和准备生丝等工序的场所。走廊下，女工拿出蚕房里或从养蚕人家买来的生丝，依次交给漂洗工、染色工和漂白工。

　　为了去除丝上的黏胶，就必须经过水煮，否则手感不好，也不易着色。洗去黏物之后，将丝一束一束放在漂白的竹竿上晾干，生丝吸水力很强，如果染色剂稍有偏差，丝卷就会残留水分，增加百分之十的重量。当时在中国、波斯、西西里，丝绸通常都是黄色的，印度有米白色、黄色和浅黄褐色的，而巴基斯坦有自然白的丝绸。

　　In a two-foot deep pond, shacks are surrounded to process rinsing, prepare for the raw silk and so on. In the corridor, female workers take out raw silk from the silkworm house or buying from the sericulture family. They send it to fullers, dyers and bleach workers in order.

　　In order to remove the sticky material on the silk, it must be boiled by the water, or it will feel bad and will be hard to dye. After washing the sticky material, they hang it on the bleaching pole to dry bunch by bunch. Raw silk is capable of water suction. If the stain deviates slightly, raw silk will remain water in it and increase the weight of 10%. In China, Persia and Sicily, silk is usually yellow. In India, it is rice white, yellow and light brown. Only in Pakistan, it is natural white silk.

Drawn by T. Allom.

Engraved by G. Paterson.

Dyeing and Winding Silk.

Teinture et dévidage de la Soie.

Färben und Haspeln der Seide.

72 卖菜船工与鸬鹚捕鱼

The Boatman Selling Vegetables and Fishing with the Cormorant

长江便利的水运为浦口的民众提供充足的就业机会。画中一个头戴宽边斗笠的菜农，嘴里叼着烟斗，一手控制船帆，另一手掌舵，用单桨控制着船前进的方向。他乘坐的船只仅用一根竹竿竖在船上做桅杆，张开着船帆，帆绳就挂在他身旁的插梢上，船上装满了准备卖掉的蔬菜和水果。

卖蔬果的农民右边，一名渔民正忙着驱使训练有素的鱼鹰捕鱼，也就是知名的"鸬鹚捕鱼"。当地渔民懂得鸬鹚的习性，为防止鸬鹚将鱼吞食，渔民会在鸬鹚的脖子系上一根稻草绳子。等鸬鹚钻入水中捕到鱼后，渔民便将它拉上船，捏着它的嘴巴，提起它的脚，鱼儿就被倒出来了。

The convenient water transport of Yangtze River offers adequate employment opportunities for the populace near the river. In the painting, a farmer wearing a wide-brimmed hat, with a pipe in his mouth, is controlling the direction of the ship and holding the helm. There is only one bamboo pole on his ship to be mast. After opening the sail, the sail rope hangs on the side of the plug. The ship is filled with vegetables and fruits for sale.

On the right side of a farmer selling vegetables and fruits is a fisherman busy driving a well-trained cormorant to fish. This is the famous saying "cormorant fishing". Local fishermen know habits of cormorants well. In order to prevent the cormorant from swallowing fish, local fishermen will tie a straw rope around its neck. As soon as the cormorant flies into the water and catches the fish, the fisherman will pull it on the boat, holding its mouth and lifting its feet to pour down the fish.

Sketched on the spot by Captⁿ Stoddart, R.N. Engraved by A. Willmore.

Chinese Boatman economizing Time & Labour, - Poo-kow.

Batelier chinois economisant le temps et le travail, Poo kou.   *Zeitersparniss eines chinesischen Schiffes, Poo kow.*

英德煤矿

Yingde Coal Mine

　　英德，素称岭南古邑，又称英州，位于北江中游。北江流经梅岭山脉，在岩石间冲出一条河道，当地矿藏丰富，人们采煤并用船向外装运。画面中的英德煤矿气势庞大，矿主砍掉周围的松树，搭起了矿工居住的小屋。

　　由于缺少机械设备，人们将矿井的平坑开凿在位于河岸的岩石上，这样矿工不仅方便进出，也方便排水，还能将煤炭直接装运到驳船上。一艘艘驳船在井口下方排队装煤，另一些则在很长的台阶下等候，由矿工挑着扁担将煤运上车，运煤车沿着人工开挖的岩石阶梯不停地上下运输。

　　Yingde, known as Ancient village of Lingnan, also known as the Yingzhou, is located in the middle reaches of the North River. North River flows through Meiling Mountains, rushing a river between rocks. The local is rich in minerals, so that people mine, load and transport by ship. In the painting, Yingde Coal Mine is of great momentum. Miners cut down pine trees around, only leaving mine workers living in small huts and offices. People are building huts on the peak, gathering many people.

　　Due to the lack of machinery devices, people dig the pit on the rock hanging over the river, so that it is convenient for workers to access and drainage. What's more, coal can be loaded on ships directly. Ships queue up to load the coal at the bottom of the wellhead. Other coal will wait at the bottom of a long step, where workers will lug the pole and load it on the car. It operates up and down on the rock ladder dug artificially.

Drawn by T. Allom.

Engraved by W. A. Le Petit.

Coal Mines at Ying-Tih.

Mines de charbon à Ying-Tih.

Kohlenminen zu Ying-Tih.

北京灯笼铺

The Lantern Shop in Beijing

19 世纪美国科学家爱迪生发明电灯之前，中国人都是打着灯笼来照明。画面是清代灯笼商的展示厅，就像一间时尚的休息室，以因应激烈的竞争。那时，一般官员的家里的灯笼非常讲究，灯笼上的图案必须随着季节而更换，因此，常见官员到灯笼店为妻儿挑选新样式的灯笼。

每个灯笼的形状和材料各不相同，球形、正方形、五边形、六角形，什么形状都有，框架有木制、象牙、金属制，任君挑选。好的灯笼师很懂设计，不论风景或人物，总会画上令人愉悦的主题并涂上绚烂的色彩。

Before the American scientist Edison invented the electric light in the 19th century, Chinese lit lanterns. As for lantern businessmen, their exhibition halls are like fashionable lounges in order to cope with fierce competitions. At that time, even the most common official family would be particular about lanterns and patterns on the lanterns must be keep pace with the season. Therefore, officers are always seen selecting the new style lanterns for their family.

All the lanterns have different shapes and materials, including the sphere, square, pentagon, hexagon and other shapes. In terms of frames of lanterns, there are frames made of wood, ivory, metal and so on. The best lantern maker knows how to design, always drawing pleasant themes and gorgeous colours about scenery or characters.

Drawn by T. Allom.
Engraved by F. F. Walker.

Show-room of a Lantern Merchant, at Peking.

Marchand de lanternes à Pékin.

Musterzimmer eines Laternenhandlers in Pekin.

临清州踢毽子

Kicking Shuttlecock in Linqing County

清朝设置的临清州位于山东省，当地有座楼高九层的临清州塔，八角锥状，底层由斑状花岗岩堆砌，墙面用精美的釉面砖拼成，每层都有挑檐，向上逐层缩小，最后优雅收顶，从下而上，可以通过一百八十级转梯迂回登顶。

临清州市民喜欢在这座八角塔之下的缓坡上休闲娱乐，有人斗鹌鹑、斗蛐蛐、猜拳、赌博，周围还坐着看热闹、抽烟袋的人群。现场还有人踢毽子，这原本是女性的活动，但男人也乐在其中，他们光着脚，五六个人围成一圈，淘汰每一轮最差的选手，最后一个没被淘汰的人就是这场比赛的赢家。

Linqing County in Qing Dynasty is located in Shandong Province. There is a Linqing Tower with 9 stories tall locally, octagonal pyramid-shaped. Its bottom is plastered by the puzzled granite and its wall is padded by the exquisite glazed tiles. Each layer has eaves, turning smaller and smaller until it ends at the top gracefully. There are 180 ladders with twists and turns from the bottom to the top.

Citizens in Linqing County enjoy relaxing and entertaining on the slope beside the tower. Some people play with quails and crickets, guess and gamble surrounded by the crowd watching and smoking. Others kick shuttlecock which used to be the female activity. Now even the stoutest men are obsessed with it. Five or six people surround in a circle, barefoot, to weed out the worst player every round. The winner will be the last one who hasn't been out.

Playing at Shuttlecock with the Feet.

Le jeu du volant avec les pieds.

Federball Spiel mit den Füssen.

76 木偶戏和皮影戏

Puppet Play and Shadow Play

　　明清时期，临清州地处京杭大运河与隋唐大运河交汇处，北及北京，西抵洛阳，南达杭州，有"繁华压两京，富庶甲齐郡"之称，人口一度号称百万，人称"天下第一码头"，是全国著名的商业大都会。

　　画面的广场上，商旅、小贩、船员云集，大家将注意力投向表演皮影戏的街头艺人。这些表演者将自制的图片放在可以透视的玻璃前，用细绳拉动图片讲述故事，旁边还有木偶戏。后来这两项娱乐从中国传到了欧洲大陆，其中木偶戏飘洋过海后，操作方式改成与皮影戏相同，演变为用绳子牵引双腿和双臂的木偶戏。

　　Linqing County, located in the beginning of the Beijing-Hangzhou Grand Canal, is not only the place where goods are exchanged and trade is made, but also the place where talents are gathered. It's common to see porters busy moving heavy goods from this sampan to another one.

　　Business travelers, hawkers and the crew gather in the square. They devote their attention into street artists performing the shadow play. These performers put self-made pictures in front of the glass that can be seen through, pulling pictures with strings to tell the story. Beside there is a bag play. These two entertainments pass from China to the European continent and Britain. The operation of the bag play has become the same as that of the shadow play after spreading overseas. It becomes the puppet show with ropes to pull legs and arms.

Raree Show, at Lin-sin-choo.

Montre des poupées à Lin-sin-choo.   Puppenspiel zu Lin-sin-choo.

通州卖茶和卖猫商人

Businessmen selling tea and cats in Tongzhou

距离北京二十英里的通州，是北京的对外港口，这里人口密集，贸易活跃，从南方运来的农产品和手工制品都在这里卸货。码头旁常有茶摊，给船工带来了方便。画中茶摊的主人站在竹竿支撑的帆布篷下，邀请路人品尝茶点，茶杯就整齐地摆在柜台上，炉子和水壶放在摊子后方。

茶摊旁，猫商正在谈买卖，19 世纪的中国，猫是桌上的佳肴，市场上贩卖的猫儿全是人工养殖而来，这对于信奉基督教的外国人而言，完全无法想象中国人无所不食的饮食文化。

Tongzhou, 20 miles away from Beijing, is the foreign port of Beijing. With active trade and densely populated, Tongzhou accepts most agricultural products and crafts from the south. Tea stalls are often set beside the port to sell refreshments to boatmen. In the painting, the tea stall owner is standing below the canvas supported by bamboos and inviting passers-by to taste refreshments. The cup is neatly placed on the counter with the stove and kettle behind the stall.

The businessman selling cats is talking about the sale next to the tea stall. In the 19th century, cats are delicacies. Cats on the market are all artificially bred. It's hard for the Christian British to imagine Chinese food culture: eating everything.

Drawn by T. Allom.   Engraved by T. A. Prior.

Chinese Cat Merchants.

Marchands de chats et marchands du thé à Tong-chow.   Katzenhändler und Theehändler zu Tong-Chow.
(Le Port de Peking.)   (Hafen von Peking.)

78 天成路上叫卖膏药

Selling Plasters on Tiancheng Road

广州天成路是个热闹繁华的商业区，在这里，赌博、抽鸦片非但不会受罚，反而成了生活的乐趣。最让外国人惊奇的，是街上叫卖神奇膏药的摊贩。这些摊贩会随身携带一张长桌，在街边将各种膏药、药罐、器具和图片摆在桌上，地上铺着纸条，写满经过治疗的病人数量和姓名。他们的口才极好，一边演说，一边表演特技，让人相信膏药有多么神奇。画中一位江湖郎中正讲解如何治疗毒蛇咬伤，旁边的助手将一条蒙着眼睛的毒蛇放进自己的嘴里，另一名助手站在凳子上，一只手抓着一条蛇，另一只手拿着专治毒蛇咬伤的解药。眼见为实，每回讲解完，就会卖出许多药丸。

Tiancheng Road in Guangzhou was a bustling and prosperous business district, with people from all walks of life gathering together. They would not be punished for gambling and smoking opium. Instead, those were the fun of life. What surprised foreigners most were stalls selling fantastic plasters. These vendors would carry a long table with them, laying every kind of plasters, medicine cans, utensils and pictures on. The ground was filled with notes, on which were written the number of patients and their names. Their eloquence was supreme. They could give speech as they were performing special talents in order to persuade the fantastic function of plasters. In the painting, a quack doctor was explaining how to treat the injury bitten by poisonous snakes. The assistant beside put a poisonous snake with eyes covered into his mouth. Another one was standing on the chair with his hat on. One of them grasped the snake on one hand, and held the special medicine for bites. Seeing is believing. Every time they finished their explanations, many pills could be sold out.

Drawn by T. Allom.　　　　　　　　　　　　　　　　　　　　　　　　　Engraved by P. Lightfoot.

An Itinerant Doctor at Tien-sing.
China.

Docteur ambulant à Tien-sing.　　　　　　　　　　　　　　Der wandernde Doctor, zu Tien-sing.

船工斗鹌鹑赌博

Quail Gambling among Ship Workers

在 19 世纪的中国，赌博在民间十分流行，无论贫富皆好此道。各类摊贩也常以博弈的方式贩卖商品，例如水果贩子会用骰子下注来销售水果。珠江上身强体壮的船工空闲时也不例外，骨牌、骰子、纸牌，喝酒时划酒拳最为常见。有些输红了眼的赌徒，有时连妻子和孩子都能当作赌注。

清代官员最喜爱斗鸡，同样形式还有斗鹌鹑、斗蛐蛐和斗蟋蟀。为了训练这些动物，许多就业机会便应运而生。画中是一群船工正开心地斗鹌鹑。

The majority of gambling, in China, was popular among the common people, regardless of the poor or the rich. Every kind of vendors often sold their products in the way of gambling. For instance, fruit trafficker would sell fruits, using dice bet. On ships in the Pearl River, it was common to find that strong boatmen played dominoes, dices, cards and punch rowing during drinking. Someone had become so obsessed with gambling that they could even make their wives and children as bets.

As for Qing officers, they liked cockfighting best, coming from the Malay. Quail gambling and cricket gambling were in the same ways. In order to train these animals and insects, many employment opportunities came. In the painting, a group of boatmen were happy, gambling with the quail.

Drawn by T. Allom.

Engraved by Ang^e Fox.

Canton Barge-men, fighting Quails.

Bateliers de Canton faisant battre des cailles.

Cantonische Schiffer und Wachtelgefecht.

80 鞭笞犯人

Bastinado Criminals

　　19 世纪的中国，各地处罚罪行最常使用的方式是打板子和杖责，王公贵族也和老百姓一样，必须接受这个制度。所谓打板子和杖责，是根据罪行大小决定次数的。犯人通常会被带到城外，在大庭广众下，由专门行刑的仆役施刑。画中两个仆役将犯人前后压制，行刑者手持六英尺长、两英寸宽的竹板击打犯人的屁股。

　　鞭笞之刑在宫廷里也被广泛应用，九品到四品的官员可以杖责下属，四品到一品的官员则由皇帝判罚。

　　In the 19th century in china, the most commonly used method of punishing crimes is the punishment of Bastinado. The nobility must accept the same regulation as peasants. The so called punishment of Bastinado is that how many times the Bastinado is depends on the severity of the crime. Criminals usually will be taken to the outside of the city, punished by professional executers in front of the public and civil and military officers. In the painting, two servants control the criminal back and forth. The executer will grasp the bamboo clapper which is 6 feet long and 2 inches wide and beat thighs of the criminal.

　　The punishment of Bastinado is also widely applied in the court. The officer ranking between the grade nine and the grade four can apply this punishment to their subordinates. The emperor takes the responsibility of the officer ranking between the grade four and the grade one. The criminal can choose to stop every five beats by begging the emperor to stop.

Punishment of the Bastinade.

La punition de la Bastonnade.　　　　　　　　Straf. der Stockschläge.

81 船过运河水闸

Ships Pass through the Canal Sluice

为了连接湖泊和河流，人工开凿的运河扮演着重要角色，中国开凿运河的方式在全世界独树一格。当船只通过浅水河段，透过水闸，运河会降低水位高的一边来抬升水位低的一边，用像台阶一般下降的河道，每下降一级，水位落差从六到十英尺不等。闸门两边的河水由卡在两侧凹槽里的木板阻隔，两道坚实的石拱将这一斜坡围起来，大船就能通过斜坡向下或向上。坡堤上有很大的绞盘，众人推动杠杆带动绞盘，运河上满载货物的船只就这样被升高或降低。引导船只通过闸门时，手持重桨的舵手站在船头，其他船员站在两边坡堤，将垫板放下来以保护船只不受损伤。

In order to connect lakes and rivers, the canal opening the sluice manually plays a vital role. The Chinese way of opening the sluice is unique throughout the whole world. When ships are passing across the shallow river section, the high water level on one side will be lowered to raise the side of the low water level. With a descending level of the river like a step, the water level gap will range from 6 feet to 10 feet. The river on both sides of the sluice is blocked by a wooden plate in the groove, with two sold stone arches surrounding the slope so that big ships can climb up and down through the slope. There are great winches on the embankment driven by workers so that ships filled with goods on the canal can be raised or lowered. When guiding the ship to pass through the sluice, the helmsman holding the heavy paddle will stand on the bow and the other crew will stand on both sides of the embankment to lay down the pad to protect the ship from damage.

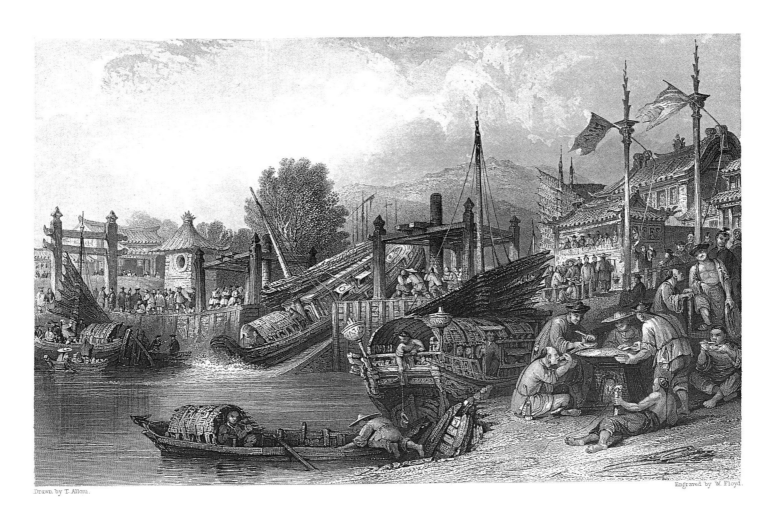

Drawn by T.Allom.

Engraved by W. Floyd.

Junks passing an inclined plane on the Imperial Canal.

Jonques passant par un plan incliné sur le canal impérial.

Böte welche einen Abhang hinunter fahren auf dem kaiserlichen Canal.

金坛纤夫

Jintian Boat Tracker

纤夫，是指那些拉纤为生的人。当年，河上百舸争流，煤、木材、农副产品和日用品全靠船只运进运出，每当逆水行船或遇上险滩时，全靠纤夫合力拉纤，涉险过关。

江苏省金坛地区不仅游客多，商船往来也非常频繁。画面中的几位纤夫裸着上半身，肩套轭具，包括一块胸板或加垫的木条，两端系着纤绳，他们合力将满载货物的船逆流拉上岸。他们的肌肉力量和身体负重可以从画中完全感受得到，他们有时一天必须工作十六个小时以上，其间无法休息。

The boat trackers were a group who lived on tracking boats. At that time, a lot of boats sailed on rivers by which people transporting coals, woods and agricultural products. When the boats sailed against the current, or met shallow shoals, they all depended trackers to pool efforts tracking boats through the trouble area.

Jin Tan, in Jiangsu Province was a prosperous county seeing a lot of boats coming and going. In the picture, people could see some trackers, barebacked, with yokes on their shoulders, pooling efforts to draw the full-loaded boat to the riverbank, and their muscle strength and body burden could apparently been seen. In many occasions, they had to work 16 hours a day and never been allowed to take a rest during work.

The Kilns at King-tan.

Chaufour à King-tan.

Die Ziegelhütten zu King-tan.

83 求签问卦

Drawing Lots and Consulting Oracles

无论是城镇还是乡村，各种庙宇寺院在 19 世纪的中国都是敞开大门迎接信徒。贫穷乡间的僧侣只能依靠施舍过日，庙宇之内无人看守。但在富庶的地区，庙宇内总有僧侣值守，民众碰上婚丧嫁娶、移居动土，都会到庙里求签问卦。求签者从一个装着许多竹签的筒内抽出一支，交给僧侣，僧侣依照签上的内容再对照卦书上的文字，为问卦者指点迷津。

此种求签问卦在欧洲人眼里并不奇怪，因为他们亦会祈求神谕。

Whether in villages and countries, mountains and peaks, secret deep valleys or inaccessible rural areas, all kinds of temples and monasteries opened their doors to welcome believers in the 19th century in China. Monks in poor areas could only rely on alms, without anyone guarding in the temple. However, in rich areas, monks were always guarding the temple and the populace would go to the temple to draw lots and consult oracles. Then monks would explain contents of lots for the populace according to words in poems of lots.

This is not special for the European because it is similar in Germany, and even British farmers will ask for lots and the Greek and the Roman will pray for oracles.

A Devotee consulting the Sticks of Fate.

Dévot consultant les baguettes du destin.

Ein Andächter zieht die Stöcke des Schicksals zu Rath.

84 从古墓远眺厦门

Overlooking Xiamen from the Ancient Tomb

画面中从古墓群往下望，可以看见厦门的全景：低洼处的城市、碟型的围墙、广阔的田野和数不清的小屋。

远眺可望见犹如内陆湖的海湾，星星点点的是繁忙往来的商船。对岸雄伟的山脉屹立，山峦呈现锯齿状，这就是鼓浪屿的所在处。这种地形刚好为处于盆地的厦门围起一道天然屏障，让海湾里得以风平浪静。航行到此地的各种船只，一年四季都可以收起风帆，停泊于此。

Looking down from the group of tombs, we can see the panoramic view of Xiamen, including low-lying city, dish-shaped walls, vast fields and countless huts. From the far distant, we can see the bay like the inner lake, dotted with busy merchant ships. On the other side, strong mountains are standing, jagged. This is the location of Gulangyu Island, forming a natural shelter for Xiamen with the basin of the terrain. It helps make the gulf peaceful and various vessels coming here in all seasons can withdraw sails and park here.

Drawn by T.Allom.   Sketched on the Spot by Captᵐ Stoddart. R.N.   Engraved by A.Willmore.

City of Amoy, from the Tombs.

La ville d'Amoy, vue prise des tombeaux.   *Stadt Amoy, von der Grabmählern gesehen.*

85 厦门古墓

The Ancient Tomb in Xiamen

当年，出于好奇心，有一支英军从厦门出发开始探险。他们在爬上一处花岗岩山丘后，意外发现山中的一处洞窟，洞窟里有一个古老的墓葬群。画面中的这座坟墓是几面矮墙围起来的，呈新月形，从形状判断，应为大官的墓。后方有一段开凿在岩石上的台阶，通向一座有着反弧形屋檐和四根木柱组成的墓门。

墓葬内部修建成阶梯式一层层排列的过道，有些空间被实心砌墙封闭起来，里面是放着死者遗骸的墓室。

Out of curiosity, several British troops set out from Xiamen to take adventure. After they climbed up a granite hill, they found a cave by accident, in which there is a group of ancient tomb groups. In the painting, this tomb is in the shape of crescent moon, surrounded by three dwarf walls. Judging from the shape, it should be the tomb of an official. There is a step created in the rock behind, leading to the gate with anti-arc-shaped eaves and four wooden pillars.

Inside the tomb were galleries and corridors built in the way of ladder-like arrangement. Some space was enclosed by solid walls, in which was tombs of the dead. Above a very long gallery, there are hundreds of catacombs opening, some of which had ashes or were abandoned.

Drawn by T. Allom.　　　　　Sketched on the spot by Captⁿ Stoddart, R.N.　　　　　Engraved by W. Le Petit.

Ancient Tombs near Amoy.

Anciens tombeaux près d'Amoy.　　　　　　　　　*Alte Grabmäler bei Amoy.*

中国的墓地

The Cemetery in China

从中国的墓地可以看出一个社会的等级划分，穷人去世后，只能建一个小小的墓，而有钱人家的墓地则是自成一格，与众不同。

画面中的坟墓就是富裕人家的，他们的后代通常用石砌或砖造结构建墓，至少有两层高，坟墓设计为圆形、多边形或其他规则的几何图形，并建有一扇相当坚固的石门以防外人入侵。整座坟墓呈现新月形，中间道路上竖起一根柱子，尖形方塔，墓前的石碑上写着死者的生卒年月。每到冬至和清明，死者的家属都会前往扫墓。

We can see a social class from the cemetery in China. Little tombs of the poor gathered together, while the rich had self-contained and unique graveyards. Their descendants were usually made of stones or bricks, at least two layers high. The design of the cemetery could be circular, polygonal or other regular shapes, with a rather solid stone gate to prevent invasion. The whole grave was at best crescent-shaped. Set up a pillar in the middle of the road like a sharp and square tower. Sometimes an urn can be placed or other buildings related to the tomb construction. If the path between tombstones is trampled, it stands for filial piety, widow's sadness and mother's grief. At the funeral, we can still see the long funeral team.

Chinese Cemetery

Cimetière chinois.   Chinesischer Gottesacker.

Drawn by T. Allom.   Engraved by S. Fisher.

87 墓地旁的掷骰子游戏

Dice Players next to the Cemetery

　　赌博在古老的中国，并没有被严格禁止，这在外国人的眼中，甚感诧异。因为在欧洲，赌徒和挥霍无度者，不仅会被厌恶，还会遭公众贬斥和蔑视。

　　但是在中国，掷骰子赌博的游戏就像看戏、放风筝、打板球、斗鹌鹑和抽签算命一样流行。画面中有一座墓地，周围是民居和树林，几个赌博的人在地上铺上竹席便开始玩了起来。可能天上还下了点小雨，有一人撑着伞在旁边看热闹，但赌徒们却丝毫没有结束的意思。

　　The gambling in ancient China was not prohibited strictly. From the perspective of the British, they were very surprised because in Europe, gamblers and the squandered would not only be disgusted but also put on the mark of public criticism and contempt.

　　But in China, the game of dice gambling is like a play, as popular as flying kites, playing cricket, fighting quails and drawing lots from fortune tellers. In the painting, these gamblers are sitting on the ground covered with bamboo mat in the graveyard with beautiful scenery and start playing. Seeing this situation, the British held the opinion that these people should commemorate their ancestors with reverence instead of releasing their evil desires.

Drawn by T. Allom.

Sketched on the spot by Capt.ⁿ Stoddart, R.N.

Engraved by J.B. Allen.

Dice-Players, near Amoy.

88 赤城兵营

Chicheng Barracks

赤城隶属直隶省，在京杭大运河的北方水源白河两岸建有兵营，规模大小与当地人口密集度成正比。兵营里驻扎的不是正规军队，而是当地民兵。当皇家船队或清朝官员通过，民兵要先放三响礼炮，仪式完毕后，再将服装和配备还给驻地的军械库。

运河上有各种船只，包括平底船、帆船、花船、小木船等，船只来来往往，常有各类事件发生，因此，赤城岗亭有警察和正规军驻守。岗亭前升起军旗，如果是满八旗队伍，旗子为正黄、正红、正白、正蓝、镶黄、镶红、镶蓝色，如果是汉族队伍，旗子中央则绘有一条金龙。

On both sides of the white river, in the north of the Beijing-Hangzhou Grand Canal, have built barracks, the size of which is in proportion to the population density or the traffic flow. The local militia is stationed in the barracks instead of the regular army. Once the population is over 100, it will become the first class. When the royal fleet or officers pass through, the militia should put three shots first to express respect. Then they should return their costumes and equipment to the garrison.

There are all kinds of vessels on the canal, including flat boats, sailing boats, little wooden boats, pleasant-boats and so on. As these vessels come back and forth, all kinds of accidents will always happen. Therefore, Chicheng barracks are stationed by the police and the regular army. In front of the post, flags will be hoisted. If the army is the "Eight Banners" army, then the flag will have seven colours: yellow, red, blue, white, inlaid yellow, inlaid red and inlaid blue. If it is the Han army, the middle of the flag will be painted a golden dragon.

Drawn by T. Allom.

Engraved by E. Brandard.

Military Station near the City of Chekian.

Un Poste militaire près de la ville de Chekian.

Militär Station unfern der Stadt Chekian.

89 大黄口炮台

Dahuangkou Fort

　　珠江沿着广州而下，两岸可见一个又一个富饶的村庄。画面中有一座落在水上的小岛，坚固的花岗岩围墙内盖了一座四层楼高的塔，墙上留有被子弹打过的痕迹，壁顶上有雉堞，方便士兵攻击、瞭望与防守。还种植了几棵大榕树，作为士兵遮荫之用，这里是大黄口炮台。

　　高塔与榕树的配置在中国非常常见，但是，对于当时的外国船队来说，却是可笑而无法理解的，因为这样的作法会让整座炮台成为显著目标，反而容易被敌军发现，并遭到敌船炮火攻击。

　　Pearl River flows along Guangzhou, and on the way we can see one after another rich villages on both sides. Suddenly in the middle of the river, an island floating on the water came into our sight. In the solid granite wall was established a tower with four storeys high. Tracks of gun eyes through the wall were left. There are battlements on the top in order to facilitate attacks, lookout the war and defense. A few big banyan trees were planted here as a shade for soldiers. This is Dahuangkou Fort.

　　It is very common to see the configuration of tall towers and banyan trees in China. However, as for foreign fleets at that time, it was ridiculous and was not understandable because this would make the whole turret become an obvious target, easily found and attacked by enemies. As a result, all the armed personnel would be buried in the fort.

The Tai-wang-kow, or Yellow Pagoda Fort, Canton River.

Le Tai-wang-kow, ou fort de la Pagode-jaune, rivière de Canton.

Der Tai-wang kow, oder gelbe Pagoda, Canton Fluss.

镇江西门激战

A Bloody Battle at West Gate of Zhenjiang City

　　镇江是中国抵御西方入侵的重要屏障，西门是当年英军攻城的主战场。北门和西南郊开战后不久，英军第二旅和海军陆战队即从陆路和水路同时攻打西门。

　　面对现代化武器装备的英军，西城守军狠狠反击，仅在 10 分钟内就击伤英军 16 名和 8 名炮兵，英军被迫退出运河。随后英军增派兵员，在强大的火力下，西门告破，但装备简陋的镇江守军不仅没有举城投降和闻风而逃，而是进行了殊死抵抗，随后在城内的小教场、高桥、范公桥等地与英军进行激烈巷战，直至全军将士壮烈殉国。

　　Zhenjiang had been an important stronghold that China resisted westerners' invasion, and its west gate was the main battle field the British troops attacking the city. Shortly after the outbreak of the battle, the British 2nd brigade and marine corps co-attacked the west gate both from land and water. Facing British soldiers equipped with modern weapons, the Chinese defended soldiers fought back seriously, wounding 16 British soldiers and 8 artillery men in 10 minutes, and forced enemies retreating from the Great Canal. But later on the British troops added enforcing units and broke the gate. The poor equipped Chinese soldiers made life-or-death struggle instead of running away. They launched fierce street fight against British troops at Xiaojiaochang, Gaoqiao and Fan'gongqiao, until all died in heroic death.

Drawn by T. Allom.   Sketched on the spot by Capt.ⁿ Stoddart, R. N.   Engraved by J. M. Starling.

West Gate of Ching Keang Foo.

91 晋江入口

Entrance to the Jinjiang River

　　在占领厦门后，不列颠舰队从晋江入海口一路挥师北上，直取晋江这一鸦片传输要道。晋江一战，英军缴获许多战利品，并控制了这一重要的通商航道。

　　在英军一路向内陆进攻时，即使清军明白该地在鸦片走私中重要的地理位置，但清朝政府的武力布置却十分简单且欠缺考虑，而这些都被一位名叫斯杜达特的舰长用画笔记录下来，并绘制成了画册。根据画中场景，在英军进攻时，清军只是做了些微的抵抗就弃枪而逃。

　　After occupying Xiamen, the British fleet went north from the sea mouth of Jinjiang River, capturing the opium transmission channel in Jinjiang River. After the war in Jinjiang River, the British army seized a lot of spoils and controlled this important channel. On the way to inland attack, the British understood that even though the Qing army knew its important location for the opium transmission, military arrangement by the Qing government is too simple without consideration. All of these facts were recorded by a captain called Stoddart and were made into a painting album. According the scene in the painting, when the British army was still far away from Qing's poor weapons and "broken copper", the Qing army just resisted it slightly, abandoning the gun and fleeing. The British army seized all the weapons of the Qing army and achieved a lot.

Drawn by T. Allom.   Sketched on the spot by Capt. Stoddart, R.N.   Engraved by C. T. Dixon.

Entrance to Chin-chew River, Fokien.

Entrée de la rivière Chin-Chew-Fokien.   *Eingang in den Fluss Chin-chew-Fokien.*

92 夺取穿鼻

Attack and Capture of Chuanbi

珠江最主要的入海口在穿鼻和大角头要塞之间，这里被视作广东这一商业中心的护城河，它的西面是一片支流众多的三角洲。尽管这片水域对于大多数平底船只来说显得太浅，但它连接了广东和澳门，也因此促成了大量贸易合作。

穿鼻之战是鸦片战争爆发前夕的中英战斗。道光十九年（1839 年 11 月 3 日）英舰在穿鼻洋（广州虎门口）进行挑衅，清朝水师提督关天培率军抗击。伤英舰一艘。英军败退，落海数十人。

The main estuary of the Pearl River is between Chuanbi and Tycocktow forts, regarded as the moat of Guangdong which is the commercial centre. Its west is the delta with great a many tributaries. Although this water area is too shallow for the majority of flat-bottomed vessels, it connects Guangdong to Macau, promoting a great deal of trade.

"The War of Chuanbi" in history is the Battle between Qing Empire and British Empire on the eve of the outbreak of the Opium War, which took place November 3 in 1838. The navy general Guan Tianpei commanded soldiers to fight back and defeated British invaders. One British ship was injured, and dozens of British soldiers fell down to the sea.

Drawn by T. Allom.

From a sketch on the spot, by Lieut: White, Royal Marines.

Engraved by H. Adlard.

Attack and Capture of Chuenpee, near Canton.

Attaque et prise de Chuenpee près de Canton.

Angriff und Einnahme von Chuenpee bei Canton.

93 乍浦佛寺之战

The War of Zhapu Temple

中国除了孔庙、寺院、先贤祠、佛寺外，还有供奉王母娘娘、火神、龙王、文神、风神、长寿之神等庙宇，对于欧洲人来说，中国的供奉模式有点奇怪，但他们对这一原则十分认同，那便是"宽容"，尊重所有的神祇。

包括中国在内，当战争发生时，宗教场所常作为临时性的避难及防御场所。1842 年 5 月 7 日英军为控制长江，封锁运河，截断漕运，以迫使清廷屈从，遂撤出宁波、镇海和定海三城，北犯海防重镇乍浦。画面中清军在乍浦佛寺的顽强抵抗被视为勇敢作战的一大证据。

Besides the Confucius Temple, the monastery, the ancestral temple of wise men and the Buddha Temple, there are some temples for the Queen Mother of the West, the Fire God, the Dragon King, the Literature God, the Wind God, the Longevity God and so on. As for the European, the worship mode is absurd in China, but they have a principle to be exemplary: Be tolerant and respect all the gods.

Including China, when the war occurred, religious places were often transformed into temporary defensive places, equipped with heroic warriors defending our family and country. Even if the geographical location of religion sites varied, they would occupy it as a strategic place as long as it is beneficial to the military strategy of infantry operations. One of the great evidences is that the Qing army resisted strongly in Zhapu Temple.

Drawn by T. Allom.   Sketched on the spot by Capt. Stoddart R.N.   Engraved by T. A. Prior.

Joss House, Chapoo.

Death of Col. Tomlinson.

Maison-jos à Chapoo. Mort du Colonel Tomlinson.   Das Haus Joss, Chapoo. Tod Colonels Tomlinson.

镇海孔庙大门

First Entrance to the Temple of Confucius

镇海县位于浙江宁波东北，坐落于甬江江口。当地的学宫文庙历经多次重修，逐渐扩大范围，变成一个庞大的建筑群，内有大成殿、明伦堂、崇圣祠和学堂等，三座宏伟大门贯穿整片建筑，最外层的大门上绘有许多图案，最为壮丽。屋顶由黄釉瓦片铺成，在阳光下会折射出耀眼金光，屋顶正中央的脊饰表现出宁波地方特色。

1841年，英国人威廉·帕克爵士命令几艘战舰从不同角度向镇海开火，约有一千五百名英军在战斗中身亡，中国的军队也损失惨重。在这场鸦片战争中最惨烈的一役后，当时的钦差大臣暨两江总督裕谦在孔庙大成殿前的泮池以身殉国。

Zhenhai is situated on the embouchure of the Yong River, northeast of Ningbo in the province of Zhejiang. Local academies and Confucian temples have been rebuilt several times. And it was gradually expanded into a great architectural complex. It contains Hall of Dachengdian, Minglun hall, chongsheng shrine, academies and so on. Three noble gates span the whole area. The outermost gate is painted with many patterns, gorgeous and gallent. A balustrade of precious wood, pierced after a regular and chaste pattern, protects the balcony of the upper story. The roof consists of yellow glazed tiles; and when the sun strikes upon them, they present the appearance of the brightest burnished gold. The bratticing of the roof's midpoint represents the local feature of Ningbo.

In 1841, Sir William Parker commanded ships to fire Zhenhai from different perspectives. It is known that fifteen hundred British soldiers sacrificed during the war. Chinese also had a great loss. It was probably the most sanguinary of all the battles fought in the Opium War. At that time, Yu Qian, who was the imperial envoy and the viceroy of Liangjiang, drowned himself to show his integrity at the Pan Pond, in front of the Hall of Dachengdian in confucian temple.

First Entrance Gate to the Temple of Confucius, Ching-hai.

Première porte d'entrée du temple de Confucius, Ching-hai.

Erstes Eingangs-Thor zum Tempel Confucius, Ching-hai.

J. MOGFORD, PINX.ᵗ

S. BRADSHAW, SCULP.ᵗ

Bamborough Castle

THE NEW CUSTOM HOUSE, LIVERPOOL.

W. H. Bartlett.   J. C. Armytage.

CONWAY CASTLE.

Frith, Photo.

J. Godfrey.

HOUSES OF PARLIAMENT,

LONDON.

STIRLING CASTLE.

THE CASTLE OF DOUNE.

Drawn by T. Allom.

Engraved by H. Adlard.

Quay of Louis XVIII, Bordeaux.

Quai de Louis XVIII, Bordeaux.

Der Quay Ludwig XVIII, Bordeaux.

Arch of Triumph. Marseilles.

Arc de triomphe, Marseille.   Triumphbogen zu Marseille.

BACHHUISEN pinx^t

Gem. Gallerie des Königl. Museums in Berlin.

W. FRENCH sc.

Making the Harbour.   Hafeneinfahrt.

The Holstein Gate, Lubeck.

Drawn by C. Stanfield.   Engraved by R. Brandard.

Andernach.

Drawn by C. Stanfield, R.A.

Engraved by J. T. Willmore

Roveredo.

W.H.Bartlett.

E. Benjamin.

Aggstein Castle.

CHÂTEAU D' AGGSTEIN.

Innspruck.

T.Allom.

M.J.Starling.

Town of Dinant.

upon the Meuse.

PETER JACKSON, LONDON & PARIS.

W. L. Leitch.   D. Thompson.

POZZUOLO, AND THE MOLE OF CALIGULA.

FISHER, SON & C? LONDON & PARIS.

H FENN PINXᵗ   G. GREATBACH SCULPᵗ

Fishing boats on the Lagoon, Venice.

C. STANFIELD, R.A. PAINTER.

R. WALLIS, ENGRAVER.

IN THE GULF OF VENICE

W. L. Leitch.   FROM NATURE BY MAJOR IRTON.   E. Benjamin.

THE PORT OF MESSINA.

Porto di Messina.

BATHS OF TITUS   BASILICA OF CONSTANTINE   TEMPLE OF ANTONINUS & FAUSTINA   COLISEUM   THE LATERAN   ARCH OF TITUS   COMITIUM   SITE OF THE ROSTRUM   ALBAN MOUNT

MEDIÆVAL TOWER   PALATINE HILL

ARCH OF SEPTIMIUS SEVERUS   VIA SACRA   COLUMN OF PHOCAS   TEMPLE OF JUPITER TONANS   TEMPLE OF FORTUNE

Ancient Rome, from the Capitoline Hill.

LOOKING OVER THE FORUM.

Piranesi.   Roberts.

St Peter's at Rome

Drawn by W.L.Leitch.

Engraved by E. Challis.

The "Scala Regia," in the Vatican, Rome.

W.L. Leitch.

J. Redaway.

THE VILLA DORIA, GENOA.

Villa Doria, Genova.

W. H. Bartlett.　　　　　　　　　　　　　T. Barber.

SYRA.

A GREEK ISLAND.

W. H. Bartlett.

E. G. Preach.

RUINS OF THE CHURCH OF THE KNIGHTS AT RHODES.

W. H. Bartlett.   R. Wallis.

AQUEDUCT OF THE GREEK EMPERORS, NEAR PYRGO.

W. H. Bartlett.

J. C. Armytage.

Harbour of Rhodes.

W. H. Bartlett.

G. K. Richardson.

PORT CONSTANTINOPLE.

W. H. Bartlett.   J. Redaway.

ANTIOCH, OR THE APPROACH FROM SUADEAH.

The Valley of Unkiar-skelessi, or the Sultan's Stairs.

In which the celebrated Treaty with Russia was signed.

FORTIFIED CLIFFS OF ALAYA, COAST OF CARAMANIA.

W.H.Bartlett.

W. Taylor.

CAMP OF IBRAHIM PASHA, NEAR ADANA.

J. Ramage.   S. Bradshaw.

ST PETERSBURG.

WILLIAM MACKENZIE, LONDON, EDINBURGH & GLASGOW

W.H.Bartlett.

C. Cousen.

Light-tower, near Coburg.

(Lake Ontario)

PHARE PRÉS DE COBOURG, LAC ONTARIO.

DER LEUCHTHURM BEI COBURG AM SEE ONTARIO.

W.H. Bartlett.   R. Brandard.

The Chaudière Bridge.

Near Quebec.

LE CHAUDIÈRE PONT PRÈS LE QUÉBEC.   DE CHAUDIÈRE BRÜCKE NÄCHST QUEBEC.

W. H. Bartlett.

16

J. Carter.

The Cathedral. Montreal.

CATHEDRALE DE MONTREAL.

DER DOM ZU MONTREAL.

Niagara

From a Photograph.

J.J.Crew.

THE QUAY, HOBART TOWN.

J.C.Armytage.

T.Heawood.

HOBART TOWN, TASMANIA.

Paul Manzoni

R. Hinshelwood

DESTRUCTION OF THE PRIVATEER PETREL BY THE ST LAWRENCE.

Virtue & C.º Publishers, N.Y.

MEXICO

Aus d Kunstanst u Publicor Inst in Hildbh

Eigenthum d Verleger

LIMA

Aus d. Kunstanst. d. Bibliogr. Inst. in Hildbh.   Eigenthum d. Verleger

T. Allom.

T. Higham.

NEFTAH, THE ANCIENT NEGETA, BEYLIK OF TUNIS.

Africa.

BAZAAR OF THE SILK TRADE, BEYROUT

Drawn by A.W. Callcott, R.A. from a sketch by C. Barry, Esq.   Engraved by E. Finden.

RUINED TEMPLE OF ISIS IN ETHIOPIA.

(At Ghertasher.)

ISAIAH. XVIII. 1. XX. 3.

Palmyra

From the Great Work of Wood & Dawkins.

Drawn by C. Stanfield, A.R.A, from a view by C.R.Wood.

Engraved by E. Finden.

TADMOR IN THE DESERT.

L. KINGS. IX. 18.

INTERIOR OF THE GREAT TEMPLE AT BALBEC.

Intérieur du grand Temple, Balbek.

RUINS OF BALBEC, A STORE-CITY OF SOLOMON.

Ruines de Balbec.

RACHEL'S TOMB NEAR BETHLEHEM.

W. H. Bartlett

R. Sands

EXTERIOR OF THE GREAT TEMPLE, BALBEC.

PORT OF BEIROUT, THE ANCIENT BEROTHAI.

Port de Bayruth, l'ancienne Berothai.

THE MONASTERY OF SANTA SABA

W.H. Bartlett.

T. Barber.

ST JEAN D'ACRE, MOUNT CARMEL IN THE DISTANCE.

Drawn by J. D. Harding, from a sketch by Las Casas.   Engraved by E. Finden.

RUINS AT DJERASH.

The Ancient Gergesha.

MATT. VIII. 28.

Drawn by C. Stanfield, R.A. from a sketch by T. Catherwood.

Engraved by W. Finden.

EGYPT.

The Temple and broken Statue of Memnon, Thebes.

"The Idols of Egypt shall be moved."

ISA. XIX. 1.

ALEXANDRIA.
Alexandrie.

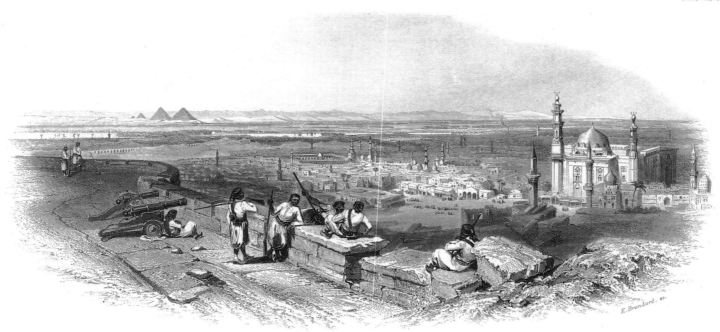

PYRAMIDS OF GHIZEH.

SITE OF MEMPHIS.

RHODA.

FOSTAT
A.D. 638.

MOSQUE OF TOOLOUN.
A.D. 879.
OLDEST POINTED ARCHES.

MOSQUE SULTAN HASSAN.
(BAHARITE SULTANS A.D. 1360)

MUSR EL KAHIRAH.
CAIRO . A.D. 973.

E. Brandard, sc.

Cairo & the Valley of the Nile

from the Citadel built by Saladin.

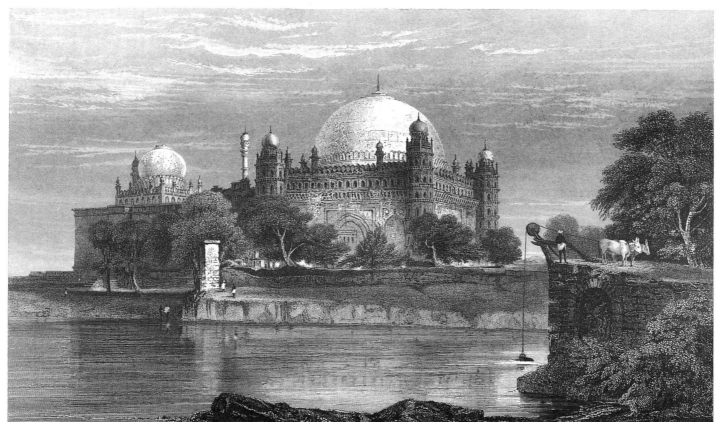

Drawn by S.Prout Esq   Sketched by Capt R.Elliot R.N   Engraved by R.Sands.

SULTAN MAHOMED SHAH'S TOMB, BELAPORE.

FISHER, SON & CO. LONDON, 1835.

Drawn by T.C. Dibden, from a sketch by T. Bacon E.S.A.

Engraved by J. Redaway

THE GHAT, HURDWAR.

TOMBS OF THE KINGS OF GOLCONDA.

Golconda is a fortified town, 3 miles west of Hyderabad, celebrated as a depôt for diamonds. A large amount of treasure is kept here by the
Nizam of the Deccan, Europeans and native strangers are not usually allowed to enter the gates.

LONDON PRINTING AND PUBLISHING COMPANY, LIMITED

Drawn by T. Dibdin from a sketch by T. Bacon, F.S.A.

Engraved by W. Finden.

MUSJID AT GHAZIPORE.

DRAWN FROM NATURE BY G. F. WHITE, 1832.

JUNGHEERA, ON THE BARREE ROCK, ON THE GANGES.

Drawn by W. Purser.   Engraved by W. Cooke.

THE CITY OF BENARES.

This City contains a population of about 600,000, and is situate on the Ganges, midway between Calcutta and Delhi.

Drawn by D. Roberts from a sketch by T. Bacon, F.S.A.   Engraved by R. Wallis.

GHAUT AND TEMPLE AT GOKUL.

Drawn by S. Cattermole.

Engraved by J. Bishop.

THE CAVE OF KARLI.

From Nature by Heine   Lith of SARONY & Cᵒ N York

JAPANESE FUNERAL AT SIMODA

From Nature by Heine

Lith. of SARONY & Co. New York.

COM. PERRY PAYING HIS FAREWELL VISIT TO THE IMPERIAL COMMISSIONERS AT SIMODA.

From Nature by Peters

Lith of SARONY & Co. New York

WRESTLERS AT YOKUHAMA

Drawn by T. Allom.

Engraved by J. Tingle.

First Entrance Gate to the Temple of Confucius, Ching-haï.

Première porte d'entrée du temple de Confucius, Chinghaï.

Erstes Eingangs-Thor zum Tempel Confucius, Chinghaï.

Drawn by S. Prout   Sketched by Capt R Elliot, R. N   Engraved by R. W. Smith

A CHINESE JUNK—CANTON RIVER.

VAISSEAU CHINOIS, SUR LA RIVIÈRE DE CANTON.   EIN CHINESISCHES FAHRZEUG, AUF DEM CANTON FLUSSE.

DIE ARCTIC=GLETSCHER
(Melville Bay)

Aus d.Kunstanst.d.Bibl.Instit. in Hildbhsn.   Eigenthum. d. Verleger.

J.Hamilton   Engraved at J.M.Butler's establishment 84 Chestnut St   A.W.Graham.

KASARSOAK, SANDERSON'S HOPE.

UPERNAVIK

(From a sketch by Dr Kane)

J.Hamilton.

Engraved at J.M.Butlers establishment 84 Chestnut St.

G.Ulman.

PARTING HAWSERS OFF GODSEND LEDGE.

(From a sketch by D! Kane.)

Engraved at J.M Butlers establishment 84 Chestnut St.

THE PACK OFF SYLVIA HEADLAND.

[From a sketch by Dr Kane.]

J Hamilton.　　　　　Engraved at J M Butler's establishment 84 Chestnut St　　　　　R. Hinshelwood

THE OPEN WATER FROM CAPE JEFFERSON.

(From description)

读 后

自 17 世纪末意大利画家加纳莱托（Canaletto）应用暗箱（近似单孔照相机）帮助的技巧，西洋画便可绘出照片一般的风景图，加上 15 至 16 世纪荷兰为印制地图而研制的刻版（开始用铜和手刻，后来用酸蚀刻和更硬的钢）印刷了大量的地图和画册。日本也产生大量利用木板雕的浮世绘印刷精品，反映了日本当时生活的实景。虽然中国在清朝时固然有写意的画和刺绣，但写实的东西则没有，没有任何印刷图画能呈现当时的生活和风景。因此，我们现在对鸦片战争年代的了解，只能从文字上获得，凭空想象吧！《红楼梦》即是最好的例子，中国可以大量印刷书籍，但《红楼梦》的插画对了解清朝初年的生活风俗作用不大。

大英帝国称霸全球的时代，也是鸦片战争之前，一直想要和中国交往，1793 年乔治·马戛尔尼（George Macartney）出使中国，见到了晚年的乾隆皇帝。使团在中国待了近一年时间，使团的画家威廉·亚历山大（William Alexander）画了许多中国人物风景（水彩），但是英国画家不知如何画中国人，因此呈现出西洋人面孔穿上中国衣服的人像。从此以后，西洋画里的中国人大多是这种样子。从景物画的写实方面来说，西洋画比当时的中国画高明很多。托玛斯·阿罗姆（Thomas Allom，本书昵称"阿龙"）的图画，对当时清代生活习俗提供了非常珍贵的数据。

从商业的立场看，这些古画在网络上都可找到，市场上值钱的只有两种：一是原始铜（钢）刻版；二是用铜板刻印的印刷原版。因为只有这两种足以真正彰显印刷的细节。本书作者能够收集到这些珍贵的历史精品，将阿龙所画的人物、景观、建筑的图片，集结成一本中英双语解说的新书，真是值得细看和收藏，也借此回顾19 世纪中国的历史和文化。

胡 伟
多伦多大学教授

After Read

In 17th century an Italian painter Canaletto painted successfully the photo-like landscape paintings by using of a kind of dark box, and meantime Holland craft men manufactured many Steel Plate engraving map and painting books in 15th and 16th centuries. (They at first cut images in bronze plate by hand, and afterward improved the technique by corroding the metal.) In Japan, there also appeared fine painting works reflecting the true situation of people's day-to-day life. In China there were painting works of free-hand traditional paintings or embroideries in Qing Dynasty, but they couldn't reflect reality and social life. So, if people today want to know the social life style in the era of the Opium War, we should only depend on imagination by reading books. For example, the novel *the Dream in Red Mansion* has possessed a lot of readers, but its illustrated paintings did little help for people to know the true social life in early Qing Dynasty.

During the Great Britain became the hegemony in the world, or before the Opium War, they wanted eagerly to contact with China. In 1793, the sent envoy George Macartney to China, and met old Emperor Qianlong. The British diplomatic corps stayed in China for near a year, and there was William Alexander, a painter in the corps, painting a lot of paintings reflecting Chinese social life ans landscapes. But the westerner didn't know how to paint Chinese person, so the Chinese persons he painted looked like westerners only with wearing Chinese clothes, and in the era, the images of Chinese person painted by western painters were always alike. In fact, the western paintings were better than Chinese ones to reflect reality, and in that regard, Thomas Allom's paintings has offered very precious materials helping people understand how the social life was like in Qing Dynasty.

From the view of business, all of the paintings could be found in the web, and only two kinds of them were valuable: one was the original metal cut plate, the other was the first printing picture in origin, because only these two could appear total detail substances. The author of this book has collected that many precious historical fine arts, published Allom's paintings reflecting social life, architecture and landscape, with both Chinese and English explanations. The new book provided us to understand Chinese history and culture, so, it was worthy to examine carefully and been collected.

Hu Wei
Professor of University Toronto

图书在版编目（ＣＩＰ）数据

印象中国十九世纪：汉英对照 / 裘国英著 . -- 上海：上海文化出版社，2018.7
　　ISBN 978-7-5535-1268-6

　　Ⅰ . ①印… Ⅱ . ①裘… Ⅲ . ①中国历史 – 19 世纪 – 通俗读物 – 汉、英 Ⅳ . ① K250.9

　　中国版本图书馆 CIP 数据核字 (2018) 第 137375 号

- -

出 版 人　　姜逸青
责任编辑　　吴志刚
统　　筹　　裘丽芳
内文设计　　汤　靖

书　　名　　印象中国十九世纪
作　　者　　裘国英
出　　版　　上海世纪出版集团 上海文化出版社
地　　址　　上海市绍兴路 7 号 200020
发　　行　　上海文艺出版社发行中心
　　　　　　上海市绍兴路 50 号 200020 www.ewen.co
印　　刷　　上海景阳画中画印刷有限公司
开　　本　　889×1194　1/16
印　　张　　18.25
印　　次　　2018 年 7 月第一版 2018 年 7 月第一次印刷
国际书号　　ISBN 978-7-5535-1268-6/J.336
定　　价　　198.00 元

告 读 者　　如发现本书有质量问题 请与印刷厂质量科联系
电　　话　　021-66288230